Data Privacy and Security - Principles and Applications

Edited by Jaydip Sen

Published in London, United Kingdom

Data Privacy and Security - Principles and Applications
http://dx.doi.org/10.5772/intechopen.1003421
Edited by Jaydip Sen

Contributors
Ajay Kumar Bisht, Hetvi Waghela, Jasmijn Boeken, Jaydip Sen, Junfeng Wu, Lingying Huang, Neeruganti Shanmuka Sreenivasulu, Rong Su, Sneha Rakshit, Xiaomeng Chen, Zhijian Hu

First published in London, United Kingdom, 2025 by IntechOpen
IntechOpen is the global imprint of INTECHOPEN LIMITED, registered in England and Wales, registration number: 11086078, 167-169 Great Portland Street, London, W1W 5PF, United Kingdom

For EU product safety concerns: IN TECH d.o.o., Prolaz Marije Krucifikse Kozulić 3, 51000 Rijeka, Croatia, info@intechopen.com or visit our website at intechopen.com.

British Library Cataloguing-in-Publication Data
A catalogue record for this book is available from the British Library

Data Privacy and Security - Principles and Applications
Edited by Jaydip Sen
p. cm.
Print ISBN 978-1-83769-676-5
Online ISBN 978-1-83769-675-8
eBook (PDF) ISBN 978-1-83769-677-2

Meet the editor

Jaydip Sen is a professor at the Department of Data Science at Praxis Business School in Kolkata, India. His research areas include security and privacy issues in computing and communication, intrusion detection systems, machine learning, deep learning, artificial intelligence in the financial domain, and adversarial machine learning. He has published over 230 papers in reputed indexed journals, refereed international conference proceedings, and 18 book chapters. He has authored four books and edited thirteen volumes. He is the editor of *Knowledge Decision Support Systems in Finance* and served on the technical program committees of several high-ranked international conferences of the Institute of Electronics and Electric Engineers (IEEE) and the Association for Computing Machinery (ACM). He has contributed to several IEEE USA standardization efforts, including the 802.16m and 3GPP LTE standards. Stanford University has listed Prof. Sen among the top 2% of scientists worldwide for the last six consecutive years (2019–2024).

Contents

Preface

In a world defined by digital interconnectivity, data privacy and security principles play an increasingly critical role in personal, organizational, and societal interactions. Today, nearly every action – from routine email exchange to a complex financial transaction – creates digital traces that hold immense value and introduce risks. As companies and institutions leverage these digital footprints for insights, innovations, and enhanced services, they face mounting responsibilities and challenges in managing the sensitivity of these data. Therefore, data privacy and security have emerged as fundamental concerns, as important as the advancements they seek to support.

Data Privacy and Security – Principles and Applications is a collection of discussions and insights that tackle the ever-changing world of data privacy and security. It brings together voices from various fields, including technology, law, and policy, offering a mix of viewpoints on essential principles, new ideas, and the rules that guide them. This volume aims to help readers understand the important issues surrounding data security and privacy while highlighting the need for real-world solutions as we deal with the challenges of our digital lives.

As we rely more on digital tools, securing systems that protect our personal information and freedoms has become important. The chapters in the book explore data privacy and security in different areas, like healthcare, finance, artificial intelligence, and the Internet of Things (IoT). Each chapter looks at important topics, covering everything from basic security practices to new ways of keeping our data safe as technology changes. Together, these chapters show how essential it is to balance new ideas with ethical responsibility in data privacy.

In Chapter 1, "Introductory Chapter: Text-Based Adversarial Attacks and Defense," Sen & Waghela explore the rising challenges posed by adversarial attacks on Natural Language Processing (NLP) systems. The authors discuss how these attacks exploit the structure and semantics of text data to mislead machine learning models. Several attack schemes, such as word substitution, character-level manipulation, and sentence modification, are presented, and their defence strategies are discussed. The authors also emphasize the need for adaptive, privacy-aware safeguards to improve the robustness and resilience of current NLP systems.

In Chapter 2, "Privacy in Federated Learning," Sen et al., discuss various challenges in preserving privacy of user data in Federated Learning. The authors focus on several vulnerabilities in Federated Learning like data reconstruction, model inversion attacks and membership inference. Several privacy-preserving techniques such as differential privacy, secure multi-arty computation, and homomorphic encryption, are also explored. The chapter also examines how regulatory frameworks, like General Data Protection Regulation (GDPR), influence privacy standards in Federated Learning.

In Chapter 3, "Privacy-Preserving Algorithms in Distributed Optimization Problems," Huang et al. address the issue of privacy preservation in distributed optimization, specifically over unbalanced directed networks. The authors introduce two algorithms, PP-DOAGT and SD-Push-Pull, to balance performance with privacy. While PP-DOAGT is designed to provide privacy over infinite iterations, SD-Push-Pull ensures privacy over finite iterations.

In Chapter 4, "Information Privacy Rights in India: A Study of the Digital Personal Data Protection Act, 2023," Bisht & Sreenivasulu critically evaluate the Digital Personal Data Protection Act, 2023 (DPDP Act) of India and assess its effectiveness in safeguarding individual information privacy. The author reviews key definitions, data fiduciary obligations, individual rights, penalties for violations, and the enforcement mechanisms within the Act. The authors also assess the adequacy of the DPDP ACT in upholding privacy rights in India's digitally connected landscape.

In Chapter 5, "One for All in Privacy Law: A Relational View on Privacy Based on the Ethics of Care," Boeken defines privacy from an individualistic and relational perspective and shows how privacy affects groups and interconnected individuals. The author proposes an approach to privacy protection that respects relationships and context, considering privacy as a collective right rather than a personal one. The author also argues that privacy loss for one impacts all.

In Chapter 6, "Enhancing Smart Grid Data Utilization within the Internet of Things Paradigm: A Cyber-Physical Security Framework," Hu & Su examine the cyber-physical security challenges introduced by the Internet of Things (IoT) integration in smart grids. The authors discuss key IoT components and potential vulnerabilities in smart grid data security and propose a dual-layer security framework with an online intrusion detection system. By enhancing data security, the proposed scheme enables the users to fully utilize IoT in smart grids.

The volume is intended for a broad readership, including students, researchers, and professionals in computer science, cybersecurity, information technology, and law. For practitioners, this book offers practical insights supporting effective data privacy and security measures. Policymakers and regulators will also find value in understanding how technical and legal perspectives on data protection intersect, enabling them to formulate policies that address real-world challenges.

As data becomes ever more critical to personal and professional life, the data privacy and security field will continue to evolve. Future technologies, such as quantum computing, will demand new standards for data protection, while innovations in AI and other advanced fields will require adaptable privacy and security strategies.

I am confident that the chapters in this book will encourage readers to consider both data security practices and future possibilities. A commitment to ongoing research, regulatory alignment, and public awareness is essential for a future where privacy and security are held to the highest standards. In an increasingly digital world, our shared responsibility to protect personal data is more important than ever, and I hope this book inspires further innovation and thoughtful approaches to data privacy and security.

I extend my warmest thanks to each author for their valuable contributions. It is because of their efforts that this book came into existence. I also sincerely thank Ms. Elvira Baumgartner and Mr. Dorian Salatic, Publishing Process Managers at IntechOpen, for their unwavering assistance and support during the process. In addition, I would like to thank Ms. Sandra Bolf, Commissioning Editor, for entrusting me with the editorial responsibility for this volume. I would also like to thank my colleagues and students at the School of Data Science, Praxis Business School, Kolkata, for their encouragement along the way. Ms. Hetvi Waghela, Mr. Rohit Pandey, Ms. Sneha Rakshit, and Prof. Subhasis Dasgupta deserve a special mention. My family has always been my source of motivation. My sincere thanks go to my wife, Ms. Nalanda Sen, my daughter, Ms. Ritabrata Sen, and my mother, Ms. Krishna Sen. Their support, motivation, and inspiration made the publication of this volume possible.

Jaydip Sen
Professor,
Department of Data Science,
Praxis Business School,
Kolkata, India

Section 1

Data Privacy Preservation Algorithms, Laws, and Applications

Chapter 1

Introductory Chapter: Text-Based Adversarial Attacks and Defense

Jaydip Sen and Hetvi Waghela

1. Introduction

In recent years, *machine learning* (ML) and *artificial intelligence* (AI) have seen extraordinary progress, leading to their integration into critical applications in various fields such as healthcare, finance, cybersecurity, and personal data protection. As these models become more popular, so do threats that exploit their vulnerabilities. *Adversarial Machine Learning* (AML) is one such challenge [1]. AML involves deliberately crafting inputs that subtly alter this input data to mislead an ML model forcing it to make wrong predictions. These threats pose serious risks to the security, privacy, and integrity of ML-based systems.

While adversarial attacks on image classification models are relatively well-studied in the literature, adversarial text attacks have attracted the attention of researchers due to the complexities of *natural language processing* (NLP) systems. Text data have unique characteristics, such as discrete tokens, syntax, and semantics, making adversarial text attacks more challenging to detect and defend against. However, with applications ranging from automated chatbots and sentiment analysis to spam filters and fraud detection, protecting against adversarial text attacks has become a critical requirement.

Adversarial text attacks can be broadly categorized into two types based on the attacker's access to the model: white-box attacks and black-box attacks [2]. While white-box attacks allow attackers full access to the model's architecture and parameters, their black-box counterparts rely only on input-output interactions. Hence, black-box attacks are more difficult to launch and they are feasible only through methods such as query-based exploitation. Text attacks are also classified based on their approach into three categories as follows:

1. Word-level substitution: This approach involves replacing specific words with synonyms or closely related terms to alter the model's prediction.

2. Character-level perturbation: Changing individual letters or characters in a way that remains mostly readable but confuses the model.

3. Sentence-level modification: This type of attack involves rearranging sentences or adding extra clauses without altering the original meaning of the text.

These methods manipulate the input without necessarily making it nonsensical, posing unique challenges to models that must interpret context and semantics correctly.

Unlike adversarial attacks on image classifiers, where continuous pixel manipulations can deceive models, text-based attacks involve discrete manipulations that must maintain the original input's linguistic structures and semantics. Furthermore, NLP models rely heavily on word embeddings that represent words in a high-dimensional space, making it challenging to ensure that minor input changes still align with the intended semantic meaning while evading detection.

These constraints mean that adversarial text attacks require a delicate balance of linguistic manipulation, often leveraging synonym replacement, paraphrasing, or intentional misspellings, to introduce ambiguity that ML models fail to handle.

2. Related work

As adversarial attacks become more common in NLP, researchers have put considerable effort into developing effective defense schemes. This section provides a brief overview of some of these mechanisms.

Jin et al. examine how well BERT [3] models handle adversarial text attacks in tasks like classification and entailment [4]. The authors introduce TextFooler, a powerful attack that successfully tricks BERT-based NLP models.

Ren et al. present a method for creating adversarial text examples by probability-weighted word saliency [5]. This technique identifies keywords in the input text that have a strong influence on the model's output and then alters them in a way to launch an effective adversarial attack.

Waghela et al. introduce the *Modified Word Saliency-Based Adversarial Attack* (MWSAA), a new method that targets text classification models by selectively altering input text while keeping the original meaning unchanged [6]. This approach improves the attack's effectiveness by using contextual embeddings and preserving semantic coherence. In another study, the authors propose a scheme for crafting adversarial text samples by combining saliency, attention, and semantic similarity [7]. Further, the authors propose a refined method for attacking the BERT model using *Projected Gradient Descent* (PGD) [8], which optimizes the attack [9].

Wei et al. introduce TextBugger, a scheme designed to create adversarial text samples by making small changes to the input text, which can lead to misclassification or unexpected behavior in different NLP systems [10].

Liu et al. propose a method to create adversarial examples that can deceive multiple machine-learning models [11]. The approach aims to keep modifications to the input as small as possible so that the altered examples are most likely able to mislead a range of models and datasets.

Jia and Liang present a method for designing adversarial samples for checking the robustness of reading comprehension systems [12]. The scheme involves making small changes to passages and questions to trigger incorrect answers from the models. This attack demonstrates how vulnerable the current reading comprehension systems are to adversarial text attacks.

Chang et al. present TextGuise, an adaptive approach for creating adversarial examples that target text classification models [13]. The attack scheme utilizes feedback iteratively from the model and bypasses detection to increase its adversarial impact.

Besides the methods mentioned above, there are several other studies done by researchers using different techniques like word substitution [14–17], word insertion

[17–19], word swapping [20, 21], phrase adjustments [22], sentence modifications [23, 24], syntactic tweaks [25, 26], and contextual changes [27, 28].

Designing a robust defense system to counter adversarial text attacks is not an easy task. It requires the preservation of linguistic integrity while having the ability to detect subtle manipulations in the input text. Researchers have carried out extensive research on adversarial defense. In the following, some of the well-known defense schemes are mentioned.

Yang and Li propose a scheme to improve the resilience of NLP systems that identifies and corrects semantic mistakes in text that have been altered by adversarial attacks [29]. The key advantage of the approach is its emphasis on maintaining the meaning of the text, which is critical for accurate text classification.

Li and Li explore how deep ensemble methods can improve the strength of malware detection systems to defend against adversarial attacks [30]. The defense strategy proposed by the authors uses a combination of several deep learning models, each trained on adversarial examples.

Liu and Lane propose a defense scheme to enhance the performance of task-oriented dialog models using adversarial learning [31]. The mechanism involves training the dialog model to create human-like responses by incorporating a discriminator. The discriminator checks the quality of the reply from the system.

Zhao et al. present a novel approach to make the NLP system robust against adversarial attacks [32]. The scheme involves causal intervention that focuses on altering the causal relationship with the input data to counteract the adversarial changes introduced by the attack.

Shafahi et al. present a method that boosts the efficiency of adversarial training of NLP systems to improve their robustness against attacks [33]. The scheme uses gradients from regular training steps to design adversarial samples, reducing the computational overhead. The major contribution of this proposition is its ability to train robust models while keeping resource usage low.

Du et al. demonstrate a strong adversarial training scheme that can tackle attacks at the word level on an NLP system [34]. The proposed approach by the authors generates adversarial examples by slightly changing words in the input text. The model is then trained on the generated adversarial samples to introduce robustness.

Huang and Chen present an adversarial defense for text classifiers by using word embeddings based on the concept of a *semantic associative field* [35]. The proposed scheme attempts to retain the meaning of the input text by embedding words in a way that highlights their connections. This makes it hard for adversarial changes to misrepresent the intended meaning of the input text.

Li et al. present a new method called *DiffuseDef* to protect NLP systems from adversarial text attacks [36]. The approach is based on the use of diffusion models to improve the robustness of NLP systems. A controlled amount of noise is introduced to the input data, which finally reduces the effects of adversarial changes.

Zhang et al. provide a comprehensive overview of adversarial text attacks and their defense strategies for NLP systems [37]. The authors discuss various methods for creating adversarial examples that can deceive NLP models and various approaches to defend against those attacks.

Wang et al. introduce *TextFirewall*, a robust defense system designed to protect sentiment classification tasks from adversarial attacks [38]. The proposed framework combines several defense strategies, such as adversarial training and input transformation, to defend text classifiers against adversarial threats.

While the current defense schemes against adversarial text attacks have shown some effectiveness, they also have their drawbacks. The adversarial training-based schemes [39] usually lead to higher computational overheads, and they may not generalize well on new types of attacks. Techniques like *defensive distillation* [40] and *gradient masking* [41] attempt to hide the model's decision boundaries and make adversarial perturbations difficult to succeed. However, these methods cannot defend against more sophisticated adversarial attacks. Ensemble methods combine predictions from multiple models for enhanced robustness [42]. However, they depend on fixed configurations and usually perform poorly under different attack strategies.

3. Conclusion and future directions

Adversarial text attacks are now a major topic of research in NLP. This focus has grown because more fields, like healthcare, finance, customer services, and law, are using *large language models* (LLMs) in their daily work. These models support tasks like sentiment analysis, spam detection, machine translation, and automated customer service. However, adversarial attacks reveal serious weaknesses in NLP systems. These attacks can reduce model accuracy, affect user trust, and raise privacy concerns. To make NLP systems safer and more dependable, effective defense methods against these attacks are needed.

Privacy is a key concern in the context of adversarial attacks. In sensitive areas like healthcare, law, and finance, systems often handle highly confidential information. If adversarial manipulation causes these models to misinterpret data, the risks are serious. For example, attacks that mislead diagnostic tools could lead to incorrect medical advice, putting patient safety at risk. In finance, adversarial attacks might trigger incorrect transactions or skew analytics, which can harm personal privacy and financial security. Defenses that protect privacy are essential to prevent sensitive information from being exposed or misinterpreted due to these attacks.

Looking ahead, several promising research areas could help NLP systems more robust. One key direction is to create adaptive defenses that can learn from and respond to new attack methods. Static defenses often do not work well against evolving attacks, so systems that can adjust themselves would improve NLP security and resilience. Another important area is using *explainable AI* [43] in adversarial defenses. This approach would help users understand why a model resists or fails against specific adversarial examples. This knowledge will make it easier to improve defenses based on how the model reacts.

Borrowing ideas from other fields, like computer vision and network security, researchers may find novel ways to protect NLP systems. Privacy-focused techniques, like *federated learning* [44], *differential privacy* [45], and *homomorphic encryption* [46], help keep data safe when training models. These methods reduce the chance of sensitive information being exposed and are hence not targeted by potential adversarial attacks. By combining these privacy methods with strong defenses, future NLP systems can be made more secure and reliable.

As more and more NLP systems are integrated into sensitive applications, ensuring that these systems can withstand adversarial attacks will become even more critical. Future research will need to focus on building models that not only perform well but also protect user privacy and adapt to emerging threats. These advancements will pave the way for safer and more reliable AI systems in everyday life.

Author details

Jaydip Sen* and Hetvi Waghela
Department of Data Science, Praxis Business School, Kolkata, India

*Address all correspondence to: jaydip.sen@acm.org

References

[1] Reznik L. Adversarial machine learning. In: Intelligent Security Systems: How Artificial Intelligence, Machine Learning and Data Science Work for and against Computer Security. IEEE; 2022. pp. 315-335. DOI: 10.1002/9781119771597.ch6

[2] Bae H, Jang J, Jung D, Jang H, Ha H, Lee H, et al. Security and privacy issues in deep learning. arXiv. 2018

[3] Devlin J, Chang M-W, Lee K, Touanva K. BERT: Pre-training of deep bidirectional transformers for language understanding. In: Proceedings of the 2019 Conf of the North American Chapter of the Association for Computational Linguistics, Volume 1 (Long and Short Papers). 2019. pp. 4171-4185. DOI: 10.18653/v1/N19-1423

[4] Jin D, Jin Z, Zhou JT, Szolovits P. Is BERT really robust? A strong baseline for natural language attack on text classification and entailment. In: Proceedings of the 34th AAAI Conference on Artificial Intelligence (AAAI'20). 2020. pp. 8018-8025. DOI: 10.1609/aaai.v34i05.6311

[5] Ren S, Deng Y, He K, Che W. Generating natural language adversarial examples through probability weighted word saliency. In: Proceedings of the 57th Annual Meeting of the Association for Computational Linguistics. Florence, Italy: Association for Computational Linguistics; 2019. pp. 1085-1097. DOI: 10.18653/v1/P19-1103

[6] Waghela H, Rakshit S, Sen J. A modified word saliency-based adversarial attack on text classification models. arXiv. 2024

[7] Waghela H, Sen J, Rakshit S. Saliency attention and semantic similarity-driven adversarial perturbation. arXiv. 2024

[8] Madry A, Makelov A, Schmidt L, Tsipras D, Vladu A. Towards deep learning models resistant to adversarial attacks. In: Proceedings of the International Conference on Learning Representations (ICLR'2018); April-May 2018; Vancouver, Canada: OpenReview.net; 2018. DOI: 10.48550/arXiv.1706.06083

[9] Waghela H, Sen J, Rakshit S. Enhancing adversarial text attacks in BERT models with projected gradient descent. arXiv. 2024

[10] Wei J, Zou K, Cao T, Chen Z, Huang Y. Textbugger: Generating adversarial text against real-world applications. In: Proceedings of the 2019 ACM SIGSAC Conference on Computer and Communications Security. 2019. pp. 1969-1986. DOI: 10.14722/ndss.2019.23138

[11] Liu F, Zhang C, Zhang H. Towards transferable unrestricted adversarial examples with minimum changes. In: Proceedings of 2023 IEEE conference on secure and trustworthy machine learning (SaTML); Raleigh, NC, USA. 2023. pp. 327-338. DOI: 10.1109/SaTML54575.2023.00030

[12] Jia R, Liang P. Adversarial examples for evaluating reading comprehension systems. In: Proceedings of the 2017 Conference on Empirical Methods in Natural Language Processing. 2017. pp. 2021-2031. DOI: 10.18653/v1/D17-1215

[13] Chang G, Gao H, Yao Z, Xiong H. TextGuise: Adaptive adversarial example attacks on text classification model. Neurocomputing. 2023;**529**:190-203. DOI: 10.1016/j.neucom.2023.01.071

[14] Qi Y, Yang X, Liu B, Zhang K, Liu W. Adaptive gradient-based word

saliency for adversarial text attacks. Neurocomputing. 2024;**590**:127667. DOI: 10.1016/j.neucom,2024.127667

[15] Pruthi G, Liu F, Kale S, Sundararajan M, Kale S. Estimating training data influence by tracing gradient descent. In: Proc. of the 34th Conference on Neural Information Processing Systems (NeurIPS'2020); Vancouver, Canada. 2020. pp. 19920-19930. DOI: 10.48550/arXiv.2002.08484

[16] Zhang Y, Qi F, Yang C, Liu Z, Zhang M, Liu Q, et al. Word-level textual adversarial attacking as combinatorial optimization. In: Proceedings of the 58th Annual Meeting of the ACL. Association for Computational Linguistics; 2020. pp. 6066-6080. DOI: 10.18653/v1/2020.acl-main.540

[17] Ni M, Sun Z, Liu W. Frauds bargain attack: Generating adversarial text samples via word manipulation process. IEEE Transactions on Knowledge and Data Engineering. 2024;**36**(7):3062-3075. DOI: 10.1109/TKDE.2024.3349708

[18] Sato M, Suzuki J, Shind H, Matsumoto Y. Interpretable adversarial perturbation in input embedding space for text. In: Proceedings of the 27th International Joint Conference on Artificial Intelligence (IJCAI'18). 2018. pp. 4323-4330. DOI: 10.48550/arXiv.1805.02917

[19] Chen X, He B, Ye Z, Sun L, Sun Y. Towards imperceptible document manipulations against neural ranking model. In: Findings of the ACL'23. 2023. pp. 6648-6664. DOI: 10.18653/v1/2023.findings-acl.416

[20] Liu H, Yu J, Ma J, Li S, Ji B, Yi Z, et al. Textual adversarial attacks by exchanging text-self words. International Journal of Intelligent Systems. 2022;**37**(12):12212-12234. DOI: 10.1002/int.23083

[21] Gao J, Lanchantin J, Sofia ML, Qi Y. Black-box generation of adversarial text sequences to evade deep learning classifiers. In: Proceedings of 2018 IEEE security and privacy workshops (SPW'18); San Francisco, CA, USA. pp. 50-56. DOI: 10.1109/SPW.2018.00016

[22] Lei Y, Cao Y, Li D, Zhou T, Fang M, Pechenizkiy M. Phrase-level textual adversarial attack with label preservation. In: Findings of the ACL, NAACL'22. 2022. pp. 1095-1112. DOI: 10.18653/v1/2022.findings-naacl.83

[23] Li A, Zhang F, Li S, Chen T, Su P, Wang H. Efficiently generating sentence-level adversarial examples with seq2seq stacked auto-encoder. Expert Systems with Applications. 2023;**213**(Part C):119170. DOI: 10.1016/j.eswa.2022.119170

[24] Moosavi-Dezfooli S-M, Fazwi A, Frossard P. DeepFool: A simple and accurate method to fool deep neural networks. In: Proceedings of 2016 IEEE Conf. on Computer Vision and Pattern Recognition (CVPR'16); Las Vegas, NV, USA. 2016. pp. 2574-2582. DOI: 10.1109/CVPR.2016.282

[25] Iyyer M, Wieting J, Gimple K, Zettlemoyer L. Adversarial example generation with syntactically controlled paraphrase networks. In: Proceedings of the 2028 Conference of NAACL: Human Language Technologies. 2018. pp. 1875-1885. DOI: 10.18653/v1/N18-1170

[26] Min J, RT MC, Das D, Piler E, Linzen T. Syntactic data augmentation increases robustness to inference heuristics. In: Proceedings of the 58th Annual Meeting of the Association for Computational Linguistics. Association for Computational Linguistics; 2020. pp. 2339-2352. DOI: 10.18653/v1/2020.acl-main.212

[27] Li D, Zhang Y, Peng H, Chen L, Brockett C, Sun M-T, et al. Contexualized perturbation for the textual adversarial attack. In: Proceedings of 2021 Conference on NAACL: Human Language Technologies. 2021. pp. 5053-5069. DOI: 10.18653/v1/2021.naacl-main.400

[28] Deshpande A, Jimenez C, Chen H, Murahari V, Graf V, Rajpurohit T, et al. C-STS: Conditional semantic textual similarity. In: Proceedings of the 2023 Conference on Empirical Methods in Natural Language Processing. 2023. pp. 5669-5690. DOI: 10.18653/v1/2023.emnlp-main.345

[29] Yang H, Li K. The best defense is attack: Repairing semantics in textual adversarial examples. arXiv. 2023

[30] Li D, Li Q. Adversarial deep ensemble: Evasion attacks and defenses for malware detection. IEEE Transactions on Information Forensics and Security. 2020;**15**:3886-3900. DOI: 10.1109/TIFS.2020.300357

[31] Liu B, Lane I. Adversarial learning of task-oriented neural dialog models. In: Proceedings of the 19th Annual SIGdial Meeting on Discourse and Dialogue. Melbourne, Australia: Association for Computational Linguistics; 2018. pp. 350-359. DOI: 10.18653/v1/W18-5041

[32] Zhao H, Ma C, Dong X, Luu AT, Deng Z-H, Zhang H. Certified robustness against natural language attacks by causal intervention. In: Proceedings of 39th International Conference on Machine Learning (PMLR'22). Vol. 162. Baltimore, Maryland, USA; 2022. DOI: 10.48550/arXiv.2205.12331

[33] Shafahi A, Najibi M, Ghiasi A, Xu Z, Dickerson J, Studer C, et al. Adversarial training for free! In: Proc of 33rd Conf on Neural in-Formation Processing Systems (NeurIPS'19); Newry, Northern Ireland, United Kingdom: Curran Associates Inc.; 2019. DOI: 10.48550/arXiv.1904.12843

[34] Du X, Yu J, Li S, Yi Z, Liu H, Ma J. Combating word-level adversarial text with robust adversarial training. In: Proceedings of 2021 International Joint Conference On Neural Networks (IJCNN); Shenzhen, China. 2021. pp. 1-8. DOI: 10.1109/IJCNN52387.2021.9533725

[35] Huang J, Chen L. Defense against adversarial attacks via textual embeddings based on semantic associative field. Neural Computing and Applications. 2024;**36**:289-301. DOI: 10.1007/s00521-023-08946-7

[36] Li Z, Rei M, Specia L. DiffuseDef: Improved robustness to adversarial attacks. arXiv. 2024

[37] Zhang Y, Shao K, Yang J, Liu H. Adversarial attacks and defenses on deep learning models in natural language processing. In: Proceedings of IEEE 5th Information Technology, Networking, Electronic and Automation Control Conference (ITNEC'21), Xian, China. 2021. pp. 1281-1285. DOI: 10.1109/ITNEC52019.2021.9587104

[38] Wang W, Wang R, Ke J, Wang L. TextFirewall: Omni-defending against adversarial texts in classification. IEEE Access. 2021;**9**:27467-27475. DOI: 10.1109/ACCESS.2021.3058278

[39] Ke J, Wang L, Ye A, Fu J. Combating multi-level adversarial text with pruning based adversarial training. In: Proceedings of 2022 International Joint Conference on Neural Networks (IJCNN), Padua, Italy. 2022. pp. 1-8. DOI: 10.1109/IJCNN55064.2022.9892314

[40] Papernot N, McDaniel P, Wu X, Jha S, Swami A. Distillation as a defense

to adversarial perturbations against deep neural networks. In: Proceedings of IEEE Symposium on Security and Privacy (SP), San Jose, USA. 2016. pp. 582-597. DOI: 10.1109/SP.2016.41

[41] Papernot N, McDaniel P, Goodfellow I, Jha S, Celik ZB, Swami A. Practical black-box attacks against machine learning. In: Proceedings of the 2017 ACM on Asia Conference on Computer and Communications Security. 2017. pp. 506-519. DOI: 10.1145/3052973.3053009

[42] Waghela H, Sen J, Rakshit S. Adaptive meta-learning for robust ensemble defense against adversarial attacks. In: Proceedings of International Conference on Emerging Trends in Business Analytics & Management Science (BAMS), and 57th Annual Convention of Operations Research Society of India (ORSI). Singapore: Springer Nature; 2024

[43] Došilović FK, Brčić M, Hlupić N. Explainable artificial intelligence: A survey. In: Proceedings of 2018 41st International Convention on Information and Communication Technology, Electronics and Microelectronics (MIPRO); Opatija, Croatia. 2018. pp. 210-215. DOI: 10.23919/MIPRO.2018.8400040

[44] Choudhury O, Gkoulalas-Divanis A, Salonidis T, Sylla I, Park Y, Hsu G, et al. Anonymizing data for privacy-preserving federated learning. arXiv. 2020

[45] Abadi M, Chu A, Goodfellow I, McMahan HB, Mironov I, Talwar K, et al. Deep learning with differential privacy. In: Proceedings of the ACM SIGSAC Conference on Computer and Communications Security. 2016. pp. 308-318. DOI: 10.1145/2976749.2978318

[46] Sen J. Homomorphic encryption-theory and applications. In: Sen J, editor. Theory and Practice of Cryptography and Network Security Protocols and Technologies. London, UK: InTech; 2013. pp. 1-31. DOI: 10.5772/56687

Chapter 2

Privacy in Federated Learning

Jaydip Sen, Hetvi Waghela and Sneha Rakshit

Abstract

Federated learning (FL) represents a significant advancement in distributed machine learning, enabling multiple participants to collaboratively train models without sharing raw data. This decentralized approach enhances privacy by keeping data on local devices. However, FL introduces new privacy challenges, as model updates shared during training can inadvertently leak sensitive information. This chapter delves into the core privacy concerns within FL, including the risks of data reconstruction, model inversion attacks, and membership inference. It explores various privacy-preserving techniques, such as differential privacy (DP) and secure multi-party computation (SMPC), which are designed to mitigate these risks. The chapter also examines the trade-offs between model accuracy and privacy, emphasizing the importance of balancing these factors in practical implementations. Furthermore, it discusses the role of regulatory frameworks, such as GDPR, in shaping the privacy standards for FL. By providing a comprehensive overview of the current state of privacy in FL, this chapter aims to equip researchers and practitioners with the knowledge necessary to navigate the complexities of secure federated learning environments. The discussion highlights both the potential and limitations of existing privacy-enhancing techniques, offering insights into future research directions and the development of more robust solutions.

Keywords: federated learning (FL), privacy preservation, differential privacy (DP), secure multi-party computation (SMPC), model inversion attacks, data reconstruction, homomorphic encryption (HE), general data protection regulation (GDPR)

1. Introduction

Federated learning (FL) introduces a new method in *machine learning* (ML) where the training process is decentralized, enabling multiple devices or servers to collaboratively build a model without sharing their individual data. This method greatly improves data privacy and security, making it especially important in our current data-centric environment where issues of data breaches and privacy are critical.

Google researchers introduced the concept of FL in 2016 to improve user privacy while still leveraging the advantages of large-scale ML models. The initial application was in the context of mobile devices, particularly to improve the performance of predictive text input on smartphones without compromising user privacy.

The introduction of FL marked a significant shift toward privacy-preserving ML techniques and has since been adopted and refined across various industries and applications.

FL is becoming more pertinent amid stringent data privacy regulations and heightened public concern over data security. Legislations like the General Data Protection Regulation (GDPR) in Europe and the California Consumer Privacy Act (CCPA) in the USA establish rigorous guidelines governing the collection, storage, and processing of personal data. These regulations challenge the feasibility of traditional centralized data processing methods, driving the adoption of privacy-preserving techniques like FL.

Moreover, the widespread use of Internet of Things (IoT) devices, mobile phones, and edge computing has led to a massive generation of data at the network's edge. FL takes advantage of this distributed data by allowing devices to collaboratively train models locally. This approach minimizes the need to transfer large amounts of data to central servers, thereby reducing the risks associated with data breaches.

Core Concepts and Mechanisms: FL involves several core concepts and mechanisms that differentiate it from traditional ML approaches:

1. Local Training: Each client device independently trains a local model using its own data. This training process can be adapted to fit the device's capabilities and the nature of the data.

2. Model Updates: After training, each client computes model updates, which are essentially the changes to improve the model based on the local data. These updates are sent to a central server.

3. Aggregation: The central server collects model updates from multiple clients to enhance the global model. This aggregation can be achieved through various methods, such as weighted averaging, ensuring that the global model incorporates the collective learning from all clients.

4. Communication Protocols: Efficient communication protocols are essential in FL to minimize the overhead and latency associated with transmitting model updates between clients and the central server. Techniques like secure aggregation and *differential privacy* (DP) can be employed to enhance the security and privacy of the updates during transmission.

Types of FL: FL can be categorized into different types based on the nature of the clients and the data they hold:

1. Cross-Device FL: This type involves a large number of relatively lightweight devices, such as smartphones and IoT devices, each with a small amount of data. The primary challenge in cross-device FL is managing the communication and computation constraints of these devices.

2. Cross-Silo FL: This type involves a smaller number of organizations or institutions (silos) that have substantial computational resources and larger datasets. Examples include hospitals collaborating on medical research or banks working together to improve fraud detection systems. Cross-silo FL typically deals with fewer clients but larger and more heterogeneous datasets.

Privacy-Preserving Techniques: FL enhances privacy by keeping data local, but additional techniques can further strengthen privacy guarantees:

1. Differential Privacy (DP): By incorporating noise into the model updates, DP ensures that sensitive information about individual data points is not disclosed. This technique provides mathematical guarantees about the privacy of the data.

2. Homomorphic Encryption (HE): This technique facilitates computations directly on encrypted data, ensuring the data remain confidential throughout the entire process [1]. HE is computationally intensive but offers strong privacy protection.

3. SMPC (SMPC): It facilitates collaborative computation of a function by multiple parties using their inputs, ensuring their confidentiality. In FL, SMPC can securely aggregate model updates without exposing individual updates to the central server.

4. Secure Aggregation: This technique combines model updates such that the central server cannot view individual updates but can still calculate the overall aggregated update [2]. Secure aggregation protocols (SAPs) are crafted to safeguard the privacy of model updates during both transmission and aggregation.

Real-World Applications: FL has been successfully implemented in various domains, demonstrating its potential to enhance privacy while enabling collaborative ML.

1. Healthcare: In healthcare, FL enables collaboration among several hospitals to train models using patient data without disclosing them. This approach can improve diagnostic models, personalized treatment plans, and predictive analytics while complying with strict privacy regulations.

2. Finance: Financial institutions can use FL to collaboratively develop fraud detection systems, credit scoring models, and personalized financial services. By keeping customer data within each institution, FL helps maintain compliance with financial privacy regulations.

3. Mobile and Edge Devices: FL is widely used in mobile applications, such as predictive text input, personalized recommendations, and voice recognition. For instance, Google's Gboard keyboard uses FL to enhance its predictive text suggestions without transmitting user typing data.

4. Industrial IoT: In industrial IoT, FL can be applied to predictive maintenance, quality control, and supply chain optimization. Devices and sensors in different locations can collaboratively train models to predict equipment failures or optimize production processes without sharing sensitive operational data.

Challenges in FL: Although FL provides substantial benefits, it also poses several challenges that must be addressed. Some of them are mentioned below.

1. Data Variability: Client data can vary significantly, creating challenges in training a global model that performs well for all clients. Techniques for handling non-IID (non-independent and identically distributed) data are crucial for the success of FL.

2. Communication Overhead: Regularly communicating the updates of model between the server and clients may lead to considerable overhead, particularly in cross-device FL. Efficient communication protocols and methods to minimize the frequency and size of updates are crucial.

3. Model and Data Privacy Risks: Despite the privacy-preserving nature of FL, there are still risks of data leakage through model updates. Adversarial attacks, such as model inversion attacks, can potentially reconstruct sensitive information from model updates. Robust defense mechanisms are needed to mitigate these risks.

4. Scalability: FL needs to scale to handle millions of devices in cross-device scenarios or large datasets in cross-silo scenarios. Scalable algorithms and infrastructure are necessary to manage the complexity and scale of FL systems.

Hence, current and future research in FL is likely to focus on improving privacy guarantees, enhancing communication efficiency, developing robust defense mechanisms against adversarial attacks, and ensuring the scalability of FL systems. Advances in these areas will help realize the full potential of FL as a paradigm of ML that prioritizes privacy preservation.

FL marks a notable advancement in ML by tackling the crucial challenge of data privacy. By enabling decentralized model training, FL allows multiple entities to collaborate on improving ML models without disclosing their data. This scheme not only enhances privacy and security but also opens new possibilities for applications in healthcare, finance, mobile and edge devices, and industrial IoT. As the field of FL continues to evolve, it has the potential to transform the way we approach ML in a privacy-conscious world. With ongoing research and development, FL is poised to become a cornerstone of privacy-preserving ML, striking a balance between leveraging data-driven insights and the necessity to protect data privacy.

The organization of the chapter is as follows. Section 2 presents some fundamental background information of FL. Section 3 discusses different approaches to privacy preservation of data in FL. Some of the existing approaches and schemes proposed in the literature for protecting data in FLs are presented in Section 4. Section 5 discusses some important real-world applications of FL in the healthcare, financial, and electronic and embedded devices sectors and how the privacy of critical and sensitive information are protected. Section 6 concludes the chapter highlighting some potential future work in the privacy in FL.

2. Fundamentals of FL

FL has evolved as a groundbreaking approach to decentralized ML, addressing the critical issue of data privacy. This section delves into the fundamentals of FL, exploring its architecture and workflow, key components, and the various types of FL.

2.1 Architecture and workflow

At its core, the FL architecture involves multiple clients (e.g., mobile devices, IoT devices, or institutional servers) that collaboratively train a shared global model under the coordination of a central server. The primary innovation in FL is that the training data remain localized on the client devices, significantly mitigating privacy risks associated with traditional centralized ML. The architecture of a typical FL is depicted in **Figure 1**. The roles of the central server and the local clients and the work flow in FL are discussed briefly in the following.

Central Server: The central server has the following roles.

- *Coordination:* The central server orchestrates the overall training process, ensuring synchronization among the clients.
- *Model Initialization:* It initializes the global model parameters and disseminates them to the clients.
- *Aggregation:* The central server aggregates the model updates (gradients or parameter updates) received from the clients to form an improved global model.
- *Communication:* It handles the bidirectional communication between itself and the clients, managing the distribution of the global model and the collection of local updates.

Local Clients: The local clients perform the following tasks.

- *Local Data Storage:* Each client retains its data locally, ensuring that sensitive information is not exposed.
- *Local Model Training:* Clients perform training on their local data using the global model parameters received from the server.
- *Model Update Transmission:* After local training, clients compute model updates (e.g., gradients) and send them to the central server.

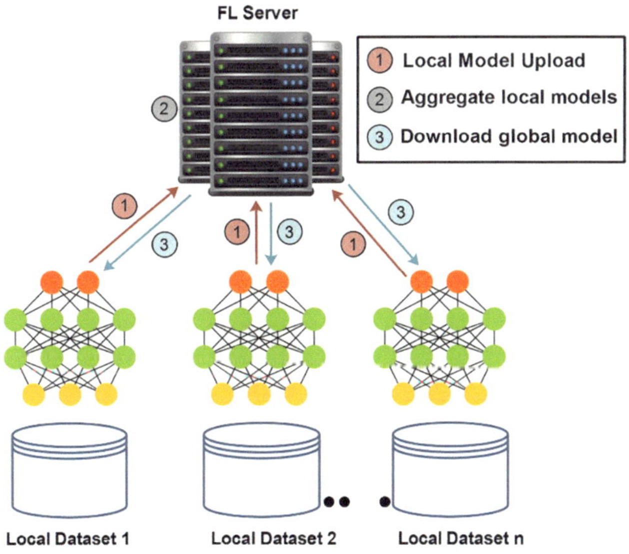

Figure 1.
Federated learning architecture (note: the figure is adapted from [3]).

- *Device Heterogeneity Management:* Clients manage their computational resources to participate in the FL process, dealing with varying device capabilities and network conditions.

Work Flow: The FL workflow involves several iterative steps as follows.

- *Model Initialization:* The central server initializes the global model parameters and broadcasts them to all participating clients.

- *Local Training:* Clients receive the global model and train it on their local datasets. This involves forward and backward passes to compute gradients or updates specific to the client's data.

- *Model Update Transmission:* After training, each client sends its computed updates to the central server. These updates typically consist of gradient information or parameter changes derived from the local training process.

- *Global Aggregation:* The central server aggregates the received updates to form a new set of global model parameters. Common aggregation methods include averaging the updates or using more sophisticated techniques like weighted averaging, considering the size of the local datasets.

- *Model Update Broadcast:* The server disseminates the updated global model parameters back to the clients, and the process repeats for several rounds until the model converges.

- *Termination:* The FL process concludes when the global model achieves satisfactory performance metrics, such as accuracy or loss, across the participating clients.

The effectiveness of FL hinges on several critical components that ensure the collaborative training process is efficient, secure, and scalable. The following components are critical for an efficient FL system.

1. *Local Training*: This involves two important components: (a) data partitioning, and (b) training algorithm. Clients utilize their local datasets, which may be non-IID (non-independent and identically distributed), meaning the data distribution varies across clients. Moreover, clients employ standard training algorithms, such as stochastic gradient descent (SGD), on their local data. The training process involves multiple epochs to minimize the local loss function.

2. *Model Update Transmission*: This involves the following tasks: (a) gradient computation, (b) update compression, and (c) secure communication. After local training, clients compute gradients representing the adjustments needed to improve the model based on their local data. To reduce communication overhead, updates can be compressed using techniques like quantization or sparsification before transmission. Secure transmission protocols ensure the confidentiality and integrity of the updates as they are sent to the central server.

3. *Global Model Aggregation*: This involves the following tasks: (a) averaging, (b) weighted averaging, and (c) advanced aggregation. The simplest and most com-

mon aggregation method is averaging the model updates from all clients. This approach assumes that each client's contribution is equally valuable. To account for varying data sizes and qualities, the server may use weighted averaging, giving more weight to updates from clients with larger or more representative datasets. More sophisticated methods, such as federated optimization algorithms, can be employed to improve convergence rates and model performance.

2.2 Types of FL

FL can be categorized based on the nature and scale of the clients involved. The two primary types are cross—device FL and cross-silo FL. These are discussed in the following.

2.2.1 Cross-device FL

Cross-device FL involves a vast number of relatively lightweight devices, such as smartphones, tablets, and IoT devices. Each device typically has a small amount of local data and limited computational resources. This type of FL has the following characteristics: (i) massive scale, (ii) device heterogeneity, (iii) intermittent availability, and (iv) privacy sensitivity. Potentially millions of devices can participate in the training process. Devices vary widely in terms of computational power, storage capacity, and network connectivity. Devices may frequently join or leave the training process due to power constraints, network availability, and user behavior. User data on these devices often include highly sensitive information, necessitating robust privacy-preserving mechanisms. Cross-device FL applications are typically found in mobile apps and IoT systems. In mobile apps, it is mostly used for enhancing predictive test input, voice recognition, and personalized recommendations without compromising user privacy. On the other hand, for IoT systems, it finds applications in wearables, home and industrial IoT systems through collaborative learning while maintaining data confidentiality.

2.2.2 Cross-silo FL

Cross-silo FL involves a smaller number of clients, typically institutions or organizations, each with substantial computational resources and large datasets. Cross-silo FL has the following characteristics: (i) limited number of clients, (ii) data homogeneity, (iii) stable participation, and (iv) regulatory compliance requirements. Cross-silo FL usually involves tens to hundreds of clients. Data may be more homogeneous within each silo but can vary significantly between different silos. As institutions have more stable and reliable participation compared to individual devices, in cross-silo FL, entities have more stable participation. However, ensuring compliance with data protection regulations, such as GDPR and Health Insurance Portability and Accountability Act (HIPAA), is critical. Cross-silo FL finds applications in healthcare, finance, and research sectors. In the healthcare sector, cross-silo FL is used in collaborative training of diagnostic models across multiple hospitals without sharing patient data. Developing fraud detection systems by leveraging data from different banks, while maintaining customer privacy is a typical application of cross-silo FL in finance. In the field of research collaborations, universities and research institutions can jointly train models on sensitive data, such as genomic information, without data exposure.

2.3 Exploration of the key components of FL

This sub-section provides more details on the three key components of a federated leaning system.

1. *Local Training:* Local training is the cornerstone of FL, as it enables each client to leverage its own data to improve the global model. The following elements are crucial to this process: (i) data partitioning and (ii) training algorithms. In FL, data are inherently partitioned across clients. This partitioning can be either horizontal or vertical. In horizontal FL, each client has data with the same feature space but different samples (e.g., different users). In vertical FL, each client has data with different feature spaces but potentially the same samples (e.g., different institutions sharing user data with non-overlapping features). Clients use standard ML algorithms adapted to the local context. Common algorithms include the following: (1) stochastic gradient descent (SGD), (2) federated averaging (FedAvg), and (3) personalized FL. SGD is the widely used algorithm due to its simplicity and effectiveness in large-scale optimization. FedAvg is a specific adaptation of SGB for FL, where local models are trained for multiple epochs before averaging. Personalized FL techniques allow each client to tailor the global model to better fit its local data, enhancing performance in heterogeneous environments.

2. *Model Update Transmission*: Efficient and secure transmission of model updates is critical for the success of FL. Model update transmission involves the following issues: (1) gradient computation, (2) update compression, and (3) secure communication. Clients compute the gradients or parameter updates based on their local training. These updates encapsulate the information needed to improve the global model without exposing the raw data. To minimize communication overhead, updates can be compressed. Compression techniques include methods such as quantization, sparsification, and pruning. Quantization, however, reduces the precision of the updates as it uses fewer bits to represent each parameter. Sparsification involves sending only the most significant updates and zeroing out small updates. Pruning removes redundant parameters from the updates. Finally, ensuring the confidentiality and integrity of the updates during transmission is paramount. Encryption and secure aggregation are two methods used to preserve the confidentiality and integrity of updates. Encryption involves the use of cryptographic techniques to protect the updates in transit. SAPs are used for aggregating updates in a way that prevents the server from having access to individual contributions from the clients.

3. *Global Model Aggregation*: The central server's role in aggregating the updates from multiple clients is vital to FL. The following approaches are generally used in global model aggregation: (1) averaging, (2) weighted averaging, and (3) advanced aggregation techniques. Averaging is the most straightforward method, where the server computes the average of all received updates. This approach assumes equal importance for all updates. Weighted averaging accounts for the size of the local datasets by giving more weight to updates from clients with larger datasets. This method helps balance the influence of different clients based on their data volume. Advanced aggregation techniques employing more sophisticated approaches, such as federated optimization and adaptive aggregation can

improve the efficiency and effectiveness of aggregation. Federated optimization algorithms like Federated SGD and Federated ADAM can enhance convergence rates and model performance. Adaptive aggregation methods that adjust the aggregation method based on the characteristics of the updates received, such as considering the variance in the variance in the updates are found to be more accurate.

2.4 Challenges in FL

As FL continues to evolve, several areas require further research and development to address existing challenges and enhance its capabilities. Some of the critical challenges are as follows.

- *Enhanced privacy-preserving techniques:* Developing more robust privacy-preserving mechanisms, such as advanced DP techniques, HE, and secure multi-party computation, to ensure stronger privacy guarantees.

- *Improved scalability:* Creating scalable algorithms and infrastructure to handle the massive scale and diversity of devices in cross-device FL. This includes optimizing communication protocols and reducing the computational burden on resource-constrained devices.

- *Efficient model aggregation:* Innovating aggregation methods that can handle the heterogeneity of updates and improve the convergence rates of global models. Techniques like federated optimization and adaptive aggregation can play a significant role.

- *Personalized FL:* Developing methods that allow the global model to be personalized for individual clients, improving performance in heterogeneous environments. Approaches like federated meta-learning and multi-task learning can be explored.

- *Robustness and security:* Enhancing the robustness of FL systems against adversarial attacks and ensuring the security of model updates. Techniques like adversarial training and SAPs are critical.

- *Regulatory compliance:* Ensuring that FL frameworks adhere to data protection regulations across different regions. This involves continuous monitoring and updating of compliance strategies as regulations evolve.

- *Interdisciplinary collaboration:* Encouraging collaboration between researchers from different fields, such as ML, cryptography, and data privacy, to develop innovative solutions for FL.

FL represents a transformative approach to ML, addressing the critical issue of data privacy while enabling collaborative model training across distributed clients. By keeping data localized and leveraging privacy-preserving techniques, FL offers significant advantages over traditional centralized models. The architecture and workflow of FL, involving local training, model update transmission, and global model aggregation, provide a robust framework for decentralized learning.

The distinction between cross-device and cross-silo FL highlights the versatility of FL in different contexts, from personal devices to institutional collaborations. Each type of FL presents unique challenges and applications, necessitating tailored solutions to optimize performance and privacy.

As FL continues to advance, ongoing research and development in privacy-preserving techniques, scalability, model aggregation, and regulatory compliance will be crucial to realizing its full potential. By fostering interdisciplinary collaboration and addressing existing challenges, FL can pave the way for a privacy-centric approach to ML that empowers individuals and organizations while driving innovation and collaboration.

3. Privacy-preserving techniques in FL

Privacy-preserving techniques in FL are crucial for protecting the confidentiality of data while enabling collaborative model training. This section delves into several key methods, including DP, encryption methods, secure aggregation, and anonymization/pseudonymization, to ensure privacy and security in FL systems. In this section, these methods are discussed briefly.

3.1 Differential privacy

Differential privacy (DP) is a formal privacy framework designed to provide strong guarantees that individual data points in a dataset cannot be distinguished from each other. This is achieved by introducing randomness into the data or computations. The goal is to ensure that the output of a computation (e.g., a model update) does not reveal whether any single individual's data was included in the input, thereby preserving privacy.

In the context of FL, DP can be applied to the model updates sent from the clients to the central server. This typically involves adding noise to the updates to obscure the contributions of individual data points. Depending on the type of noise being added and the way the noise is added, different types of DP may be implemented as discussed in the following.

Noise addition: Each client adds noise to its computed gradients or parameter updates before sending them to the central server. The noise is typically drawn from a statistical distribution, such as a Gaussian or Laplace distribution, with a scale determined by a privacy parameter (epsilon, ε). A smaller ε indicates stronger privacy guarantees but may reduce the utility of the model.

Local Differential Privacy: This approach ensures that each client's data remains private even before aggregation. The noise added at the client level is calibrated to provide DP guarantees. This method protects against adversaries who might intercept updates during transmission.

Global Differential Privacy: In some cases, noise is added at the server level after aggregating the updates from all clients. This ensures that the aggregated update meets DP guarantees, though it may require trusting the server to some extent.

Advantages and Challenges in DP: DP provides two advantages: (i) strong privacy guarantees and (ii) flexibility. DP provides mathematically proven rigorous privacy guarantees and it can be adjusted to trade-off between privacy and model accuracy. However, there are some challenges which include: (i) accuracy vs. privacy trade-off and (ii) hyperparameter tuning. Adding noise can degrade the model's performance, especially if the privacy requirements are stringent. Selecting appropriate noise scales and privacy parameters requires careful tuning and domain knowledge.

3.2 Encryption methods

Encryption methods are essential for ensuring that data and model updates remain confidential during transmission and computation. Two prominent techniques in FL are *HE* and *secure multi-party computation*. These techniques are discussed briefly in the following.

1. *Homomorphic Encryption*: HE is a type of encryption that allows computations to be performed on ciphertexts (encrypted data) without needing to decrypt them. The result of the computation remains encrypted and can be decrypted later to obtain the correct result. HE in FL involves three fundamental steps: (i) encryption of updates, (ii) aggregation of encrypted updates, and (iii) decryption. Clients encrypt their model updates using an HE scheme before sending them to the central server. Common schemes include partially HE (PHE) and fully HE (FHE). The central server aggregates the encrypted updates directly, performing operations like addition and multiplication on the ciphertexts. As the operations are homomorphic, the result is an encrypted aggregate that can be decrypted by an authorized party. After aggregation, the server or a trusted third party decrypts the aggregated results to obtain the updated global model.

Advantages and Challenges in DP: Confidentiality and security are the two distinct advantages of HE. HE ensures that updates remain confidential throughout the computation process. It also protects against external adversaries and malicious servers. However, there are challenges associated with HE too. Two important challenges are (i) high computational overhead and (ii) high complexity. HE schemes, particularly FHE, can be computationally intensive and slow. Moreover, implementing HE requires significant expertise and careful handling of cryptographic parameters.

2. *Secure Multiparty Computation (SMPC)*: SMPC allows multiple parties to jointly compute a function over their inputs while keeping those inputs private. The computation is structured so that no party learns anything about the other parties' inputs beyond what can be inferred from the output. SMPC involves three steps in its operation in FL. These steps are (i) secret sharing, (ii) distributed computation, and (iii)reconstruction. Each client splits its model updates into multiple shares and distributes them among the participating parties (including the central server and other clients). The parties collectively perform the aggregation on the shares. No single party has enough information to reconstruct the original updates during the computation. After computation, the shares are combined to obtain the aggregated update, which is then used to update the global model.

Advantages and Challenges in SMPC: The primary advantages of SMPC are (i) high level of privacy and (ii) no need of trusted environment. SMPC ensures that no individual party learns the complete updates from any other party. It also reduces the need to trust any single party, enhancing overall security. However, SMPC has its own challenges too. SMPC typically requires significant communication between parties, which can be a bottleneck. Moreover, designing and implementing SMPC protocols is complex and requires careful coordination.

3.3 Secure aggregation

Secure aggregation is a technique designed to aggregate model updates in such a way that the central server cannot see individual contributions. Instead, it only sees the aggregated result, ensuring the privacy of individual updates. In FL, SAPs work in three steps: (i) encryption of updates, (ii) aggregation of encrypted updates, and (iii) decryption. In the first step, each client encrypts its model updates using a secure encryption scheme before sending them to the central server. In the second step, the central server aggregates the encrypted updates. The protocol ensures that the server can only decrypt and aggregated result and not the individual updates. In the third and final step, the aggregated update is decrypted, providing the global model update without revealing individual contributions.

The implementation of SAPs involves two initial steps: (i) pairwise masking and (ii) additive secret sharing. In the pairwise masking phase, each client generates a random mask and shares it with other clients using a secure channel. The masks are used to obfuscate the updates before sending them to the server. The server aggregates the masked updates, and the masks cancel out in the aggregation process, revealing the aggregated results. In the additive secret sharing phase, each update is split into multiple shares, and the shares are distributed among multiple servers or parties. The servers perform the aggregation on the shares, ensuring that no single server learns the individual updates.

Advantages and Challenges in Secure Aggregation: Secure aggregation has two distinct advantages: (i) enhanced privacy and (ii) higher efficiency. Secure aggregation ensures that the server cannot see individual updates, enhancing privacy. Moreover, compared to full HE or SMPC, secure aggregation can be more efficient in terms of computation and communication overheads. Higher complexity and a lack of robustness are two challenges for secure aggregation. Implementing SAPs requires careful design and coordination among clients. Additionally, the protocol must handle cases where some clients drops out of behave maliciously.

3.4 Anonymization and pseudonymization

Anonymization and pseudonymization are techniques used to obscure personal identifiers in data, making it difficult to link data back to specific individuals. While these techniques are commonly used in data privacy, they also play a role in FL to enhance the privacy of participants.

Anonymization: Anonymization encompasses various techniques including data anonymization, K-anonymity, and L-diversity. Data anonymization involves removing or altering personal identifiers, such as names, addresses, and other unique attributes, to prevent the data from being traced back to individuals. K-anonymity ensures that each record in the dataset is indistinguishable from at least K-1 other records based on certain identifying attributes, thereby minimizing the risk of re-identification. L-diversity builds on K-anonymity by ensuring that each group of similar records (equivalence class) contains at least L different values for sensitive attributes, offering enhanced protection against attribute disclosure.

Pseudonymization: In data pseudonymization, identifiers are replaced with pseudonyms or tokens that can only be linked back to the original identifiers using a separate mapping table. This ensure that data analysis can be performed without revealing personal identifiers. Unlike anonymization, pseudonymization is reversible, allowing data to be reidentified, if necessary, using the mapping table.

Advantages and Challenges in Anonymization and Pseudonymization: There are two advantages for these two approaches: (i) enhanced privacy and (ii) compliance with standards. Anonymization and pseudonymization protect personal identifiers. Moreover, these techniques help in meeting regulatory requirements for data protection, such as GDPR and HIPAA. However, there are challenges too. Anonymization can lead to loss of data utility, making it harder to perform certain analyses. Again, pseudonymization is reversible, which means it requires secure handling of the mapping table to prevent data breaches.

Privacy-preserving techniques in FL are essential for ensuring the confidentiality and security of data while enabling collaborative model training. DP, encryption methods like HE and secure multi-party computation, secure aggregation, and anonymization/pseudonymization each plays a crucial role in protecting privacy.

DP provides strong mathematical guarantees by adding noise to model updates, ensuring that individual data points remain indistinguishable. Encryption methods like HE allow computations on encrypted data, while SMPC enables collaborative computation without data leakage. SAPs ensure that the server can only see the aggregated result, not individual updates. Anonymization and pseudonymization techniques obscure personal identifiers, further enhancing privacy and compliance with data protection regulations.

Each technique has its own benefits and challenges, and their implementation involves balancing trade-offs between privacy, utility, and computational overhead. As FL continues to evolve, ongoing research and development in these privacy-preserving techniques will be crucial to addressing existing challenges and enhancing the security and effectiveness of FL systems.

4. Existing methods of privacy in FL

Privacy in FL (FL) has become a significant area of research due to the sensitive nature of data involved and the increasing concern over data privacy. This section surveys important existing works that have addressed privacy issues in FL, encompassing various techniques and methodologies. We will explore DP, encryption methods, SAPs, and other privacy-preserving mechanisms that have been proposed or implemented in FL.

4.1 Differential privacy in FL

In this section, some DP-based privacy scheme for FL are discussed in details.

McMahan et al. introduce a method for training recurrent language models using DP within the FL framework [4]. The authors propose using differentially private stochastic gradient descent (DP-SGD) to ensure that individual user data remains protected and cannot be reverse-engineered from the trained model. By introducing noise adding noise into model updates, this method provides DP guarantees while trading-off privacy with the accuracy of model. Demonstrated on a language modeling task, the technique predicts the next word in a sequence based on previous words, enabling collaborative learning from a large user base while maintaining text data privacy.

Abadi et al. presents a framework for training deep learning models with strong privacy guarantees using DP [5]. The authors introduce *differentially private stochastic gradient descent* (DP-SGD), which adds carefully calibrated noise to the gradients during the training process to ensure that individual data points cannot be identified. The scheme introduces privacy accounting techniques that track the cumulative privacy loss over multiple training iterations, known as the privacy budget. Empirical results demonstrate the effectiveness of DP-SGD on various computationally intensive tasks based on deep learning.

Geyer et al. propose a novel scheme integrating DP into FL at the client level [6]. The authors propose adding noise to the updates from each client before they are aggregated, ensuring that the central server cannot infer information about any individual client's data. The authors also provide a comprehensive analysis of the privacy budget and its implications on model performance.

Fu et al. provide an analysis of the integration of DP in FL to improve security and privacy of data [7]. The authors systematically review existing methodologies that combine DP techniques with FL frameworks, addressing the inherent privacy risks. They also discuss how DP ensures that the inclusion or exclusion of any single participant's data does not significantly alter the results protecting data privacy. The work categorizes various approaches based on their implementation strategies, such as noise addition, gradient perturbation, and secure aggregation. The authors also provide a critical evaluation of the scalability and efficiency of these methods, considering the computational and communication overheads involved.

Gu et al. investigate how the integration of DP affects the fairness of ML models in FL settings [8]. The authors explore the tension between ensuring privacy and maintaining model fairness, highlighting that privacy-preserving techniques can inadvertently introduce biases. They systematically analyze the impact of DP on model performance across different demographic groups, identifying potential disparities. Their findings suggest that while DP effectively protects individual data, it can also exacerbate inequalities in model predictions, leading to unfair outcomes for certain groups. The work also discusses various metrics for assessing fairness and evaluates the trade-offs involved in balancing privacy and fairness. The authors propose methods to mitigate the adverse effects on fairness, such as adaptive noise mechanisms and fairness-aware training algorithms.

Li et al. present an advanced framework for improving the privacy of FL systems [9]. The proposition includes a novel optimization scheme that integrates DP to protect individual user data during the collaborative training process. By introducing an adaptive noise mechanism, the framework dynamically adjusts the noise added to the updates, to optimally trade-off privacy and accuracy of models. This approach mitigates the performance degradation typically associated with DP. The work also introduces a SAP to ensure that only the aggregated results are accessible, further safeguarding individual contributions. Experimental evaluations on various datasets demonstrate that their optimized scheme significantly improves model performance while maintaining strong privacy protection.

Löbner et al. explore the application of *local DP* (LDP) to protect user data in FL scenarios, specifically for email classification tasks [10]. A new scheme is proposed that integrates LDP into the FL process, ensuring that users' raw data remains private even before it is transmitted for aggregation. By applying noise to the data at the local level, their method prevents sensitive information from being exposed during model training. The framework effectively addresses privacy concerns inherent in FL, in which a model is trained in a collaboratively way using data from multiple sources.

The work presents a detailed analysis of the trade-offs between privacy and model accuracy, demonstrating that their approach maintains high classification performance while providing robust privacy guarantees. Experimental results on email datasets illustrate that the LDP-enhanced FL model can achieve competitive accuracy compared to traditional methods.

Wei et al. delve into the development and evaluation of DP-enhanced algorithms for FL [11]. The authors propose a suite of algorithms that incorporate DP mechanisms to safeguard individual data contributions during the FL process. The trading-off of privacy and accuracy of models has been done ensuring that the utility of the trained models remains high while providing strong privacy guarantees. The work details the mathematical foundations of the proposed algorithms, including the specific noise addition techniques used to achieve DP. Through comprehensive theoretical analysis, the authors establish the privacy guarantees and performance bounds of their algorithms. They also present extensive empirical evaluations on various benchmark datasets, demonstrating that their methods maintain competitive accuracy compared to non-private FL approaches. The results highlight the effectiveness of their algorithms in mitigating privacy risks without significantly degrading model performance.

Li et al. introduce a novel approach that combines FL with transfer learning while incorporating DP to protect sensitive data [12]. The authors aim to address the challenge of training models collaboratively across different organizations that have diverse datasets, without compromising privacy. Their framework leverages transfer learning to enable knowledge transfer from a source domain to a target domain within a FL setup. To ensure privacy, they integrate DP mechanisms, adding noise to the model updates to prevent the exposure of individual data points. This combination allows organizations to benefit from shared knowledge without the need to share raw data, preserving both privacy and data utility. The work also provides a theoretical analysis of the privacy guarantees and evaluates the performance of the proposed method through experiments on real-world datasets. The results demonstrate that their approach maintains high model accuracy while providing strong privacy protection.

Park & Choi explore the integration of DP in FL systems that utilize *over-the-air computation* (OAC) [13]. The scheme exploits the inherent properties of OAC to enhance privacy and efficiency in FL. By combining OAC with DP, the framework ensures that individual data contributions remain confidential during the aggregation process. The approach uses OAC to simultaneously aggregate updates from multiple devices over a wireless channel, adding noise to the aggregated signal to achieve DP. This scheme has a reduced overhead of computing and communication making it scalable for large-scale FL deployments.

4.2 Encryption methods in FL

Encryption methods play a vital role in securing data during the FL process. This section discusses some encryption-based schemes for FL privacy.

Keith Bonawitz et al. introduces a protocol designed to enhance privacy in FL by securely aggregating user-held data [14]. The authors address the challenge of ensuring that individual users' data remains confidential while still enabling the collective training of a ML model. Their approach uses cryptographic techniques to perform secure aggregation, ensuring that only the aggregated results are revealed, not the individual contributions. This is achieved through a combination of HE and secret sharing, which allows the aggregation process to be both secure and efficient. The protocol is robust against dropouts, meaning it can handle the scenario where some users do not complete the training process. Furthermore, it is designed to be scalable, accommodating many participants with minimal overhead.

Truex et al. explore the integration of several privacy-preserving schemes for FL to enhance the security and efficiency [15]. The authors recognize that no single approach is sufficient to address all privacy and scalability challenges, thus advocating for hybrid solutions. They combine DP, secure multiparty computation, and HE to protect sensitive data during the FL process. Secure multiparty computation enables multiple parties to collaboratively compute a function value based on their individual inputs which are private to them. HE allows computations to be carried out on encrypted data without needing decryption. The work also discusses the several optimization techniques for trade-offs computing and communication overhead with the level of privacy achieved.

Phong et al. revisit existing methods and propose enhancements to strengthen the privacy of deep learning models [16]. The authors address the challenge of protecting sensitive data during the training process by leveraging advanced cryptographic techniques. They build upon HE to allow computations on encrypted data, ensuring that data privacy is maintained without exposing underlying information. The proposed enhancements focus on optimizing the encryption schemes to mitigate the significant computational overhead typically associated with HE. By doing so, they make privacy-preserving deep learning more practical for real-world applications. The paper also introduces methods to maintain model accuracy while ensuring privacy, balancing the trade-offs between privacy protection, accuracy, and computational efficiency.

Park and Lim explore the implementation of privacy-preserving FL (FL) using HE [17]. The authors propose a method ensures that sensitive information remains secure during the training process. They also address the challenges associated with integrating HE into FL, such as computational overhead and communication costs. To tackle these, the authors propose optimizations that balance privacy, efficiency, and accuracy. Detailed experimental results demonstrating the feasibility and effectiveness of the proposed approach are also presented.

Kurniawan & Mambo investigates the use of HE to enhance privacy preservation in FL, specifically for deep active learning (DAL) scenarios [18]. The proposed technique ensures data privacy is protected during model training. The authors identify several challenges of applying HE in the context of deep active learning, such as increased computational demands and communication overhead. The work also proposes several optimizations to mitigate these challenges, balancing security with efficiency and performance. Experimental results validate the feasibility and effectiveness of their approach, demonstrating that it can maintain high levels of data privacy without significantly compromising the learning outcomes. The authors' method provides a practical solution for secure collaborative learning, particularly in environments where data sensitivity is a primary concern.

Nguyen & Thai addresses the critical issue of preserving privacy and security in FL [19]. The authors examine various privacy and security threats inherent in FL, such as data leakage, model inversion attacks, and malicious participants. They propose a comprehensive framework that incorporates multiple techniques to mitigate these risks, including DP, secure multi-party computation, and robust aggregation methods. The framework proposed by the authors aims to protect both the data and the model parameters during the training process. Experimental evaluations demonstrate the effectiveness of the proposed framework in maintaining privacy and security without significantly degrading model performance.

Gao et al. explore strategies for ensuring privacy and reliability in decentralized FL [20]. The authors address critical issues related to privacy preservation and reliability in FL environments. They propose a novel framework that integrates privacy-preserving techniques such as DP and secure multiparty computation to safeguard sensitive data during the learning process. Additionally, the framework incorporates mechanisms to enhance reliability, ensuring the robustness of the FL system against potential failures and malicious attacks. The proposed methods are designed to protect both the data and model integrity, thereby enhancing the overall security of the system. Experimental results validate the effectiveness of the framework, demonstrating that it can maintain high levels of privacy and reliability without compromising the performance of the learning model.

Mothukuri et al. present a comprehensive survey on the security and privacy challenges in FL [21]. The authors systematically review the various security and privacy threats that can affect FL, such as data poisoning, backdoor attacks, and inference attacks. They discuss existing defense mechanisms, including DP, secure multiparty computation, and HE, highlighting their strengths and limitations. The survey also explores the balance between model performance and the robustness of these security measures. The authors emphasize the importance of designing scalable and efficient solutions to address the evolving threats in FL environments. They identify gaps in the current research and suggest potential directions for future work to enhance the security and privacy of FL.

Zhao et al. address the challenge of maintaining efficiency and privacy in FL while defending against poisoning adversaries [22]. The decentralized nature of FL makes it vulnerable to poisoning attacks, where malicious participants can corrupt the model by injecting false data. The authors propose a robust framework that combines privacy-preserving techniques with mechanisms to detect and mitigate poisoning attacks. Their approach employs DP to protect individual data contributions and integrates anomaly detection algorithms to identify and exclude malicious updates. Experimental evaluations demonstrate the effectiveness of the proposed methods in enhancing both the security and accuracy of FL models.

Wang et al. introduce VOSA, a framework designed to enhance privacy-preserving FL through verifiable and oblivious secure aggregation [23]. FL enables collaborative model training across decentralized devices, ensuring data privacy by keeping data local. However, the aggregation of local updates poses privacy risks and requires secure methods to prevent data leakage. VOSA addresses these concerns by integrating secure aggregation techniques with verifiable computation, ensuring that the aggregated results are both accurate and privacy-preserving. The framework leverages cryptographic protocols to perform oblivious aggregation, meaning that the server cannot learn individual contributions. Additionally, VOSA includes mechanisms for participants to verify the correctness of the aggregation process, enhancing trust and reliability. Experimental results demonstrate that VOSA effectively maintains privacy and security without significantly impacting the efficiency of the FL process.

4.3 Secure aggregation protocols (SAPs)

SAPs ensure that the central server can aggregate model updates without accessing individual updates, providing a layer of security that protects user data.

Zhao et al. introduces SEAR, a novel framework designed to enhance the security and efficiency of FL in the presence of Byzantine adversaries [24]. The authors address the challenge of maintaining robust model performance when some participants may act maliciously or send incorrect data. SEAR combines secure aggregation techniques with Byzantine-robust algorithms to ensure that the aggregation process is both confidential and resilient to adversarial behavior. The framework employs cryptographic methods to protect data during transmission, ensuring that individual contributions remain private. Additionally, SEAR incorporates robust aggregation rules that can effectively identify and mitigate the impact of malicious participants. The authors provide a detailed analysis of SEAR's theoretical security guarantees and its practical performance.

So et al. present an innovative approach to overcoming the computational inefficiencies associated with secure aggregation in FL [25]. The authors introduce TURBO-AGGREGATE, a novel protocol designed to reduce the quadratic communication and computation costs that typically hinder scalable secure FL. This protocol leverages advanced cryptographic techniques to enable efficient aggregation while maintaining strong privacy guarantees for individual users' data. TURBO-AGGREGATE achieves its efficiency by using a hybrid approach that combines HE with a secure shuffling mechanism, significantly reducing the overhead compared to traditional methods. The authors provide a rigorous theoretical analysis of the protocol's security and performance, demonstrating that it can securely aggregate data with linear communication complexity.

Rathee et al. introduce ELSA, a secure aggregation framework for FL designed to withstand the presence of malicious actors [26]. FL allows multiple devices to collaboratively train a model without sharing their local data, preserving privacy. However, the aggregation process is vulnerable to attacks from malicious participants who may attempt to disrupt the learning process or infer sensitive information. ELSA addresses these issues by incorporating cryptographic techniques to securely aggregate model updates while ensuring that the contributions of individual participants remain confidential. The framework uses a combination of HE and zero-knowledge proofs to provide strong privacy guarantees and detect any malicious behavior. Experimental results demonstrate that ELSA effectively secures the aggregation process, maintaining model accuracy even in the presence of adversarial actors.

Fereidooni et al. introduces SAFELearn, a framework aimed at ensuring secure aggregation in private FL [27]. The authors argue that the aggregation of local model updates poses a significant risk of data leakage. SAFELearn addresses this by employing cryptographic techniques to securely aggregate the updates while ensuring that individual data contributions remain confidential. The framework leverages HE and secure multiparty computation to provide strong privacy guarantees. It also includes mechanisms to verify the integrity of the aggregated results, enhancing the overall security of the learning process. Experimental evaluations show that SAFELearn maintains model accuracy and efficiency while providing robust protection against data breaches.

Zhong et al. introduce WVFL, a framework for weighted verifiable secure aggregation in FL [28]. In FL, the aggregation of model updates is vulnerable to data leakage and tampering. WVFL addresses these issues by incorporating secure aggregation techniques with weighted updates to reflect the varying importance of different participants' data. The framework employs cryptographic protocols to ensure that the aggregation process is both secure and verifiable, preventing malicious actors from tampering with the results. Additionally, WVFL includes mechanisms to verify the correctness of the aggregated updates, enhancing trust and reliability. Experimental results demonstrate that WVFL effectively maintains the privacy and security of the aggregated data while preserving model accuracy and efficiency.

Zhou et al. present a comprehensive survey on security aggregation techniques, focusing on their application in various domains including FL and distributed systems [29]. Aggregation plays a critical role in combining data or computations from multiple sources while preserving confidentiality and integrity. The authors systematically review different approaches to secure aggregation, such as cryptographic methods like HE, secure multiparty computation, and zero-knowledge proofs. They discuss the strengths and limitations of each technique in ensuring data privacy and preventing attacks such as data leakage and manipulation. The survey also explores recent advancements and emerging trends in secure aggregation, highlighting their implications for improving the robustness and efficiency of distributed systems.

Sami and Güler explore the implementation of secure aggregation specifically tailored for clustered FL [30]. The aggregation of model updates in FL can be vulnerable to privacy breaches and attacks from malicious participants. The authors propose a novel framework that introduces clustering techniques to enhance both the efficiency and security of aggregation in federated settings. Their approach leverages cryptographic protocols such as HE and SMPC to ensure that model updates from clustered devices are aggregated securely without revealing individual contributions. The framework also includes mechanisms for verifying the integrity and authenticity of the aggregated results, thereby enhancing trust and reliability in the FL process. Experimental evaluations demonstrate that their method effectively balances privacy, security, and computational efficiency, making it suitable for practical deployment in clustered FL scenarios.

Liu et al. address the challenge of fast and secure aggregation in privacy-preserving FL [31]. The method aims to accelerate the aggregation process without compromising privacy. It leverages cryptographic techniques such as HE and SMPC to ensure that aggregated results remain confidential and accurate. The framework includes optimizations to reduce computational overhead, enabling efficient aggregation even with a large number of participating devices. Experimental results demonstrate that their method achieves significant improvements in aggregation speed while maintaining robust privacy guarantees.

Truong et al. present a comprehensive survey focused on privacy preservation in FL, specifically examining it through the lens of GDPR [32]. The authors systematically review the challenges and strategies related to privacy in FL emphasizing GDPR compliance as a critical consideration for data protection in European contexts. They discuss various privacy-preserving techniques employed in FL, including DP, FL-specific encryption methods, and anonymization techniques. The survey highlights the intersection of FL with GDPR principles such as data minimization, purpose limitation, and accountability, providing insights into how FL systems can align with regulatory requirements. Additionally, the authors explore emerging trends and future directions for enhancing privacy in FL systems under GDPR guidelines.

Li et al. provide a comprehensive survey on data security and privacy-preserving techniques in FL tailored for the edge and IoT environments [33]. The authors systematically review the unique challenges and existing solutions related to data security and privacy in FL at the edge and IoT levels. They discuss various security threats such as data leakage, inference attacks, and model poisoning, emphasizing the vulnerabilities inherent in edge devices with limited resources. The survey covers a range of privacy-preserving techniques applicable to FL, including DP, HE, secure aggregation, and FL-specific optimizations. Furthermore, the authors examine the integration of these techniques with edge computing paradigms to enhance both security and efficiency in FL systems.

4.4 Anonymization and pseudonymization techniques

Anonymization and pseudonymization are crucial for protecting personal identifiers in data, ensuring that sensitive information cannot be traced back to individuals.

Shokri & Shmatikov introduce a pioneering approach to training deep learning models on private data without compromising individual privacy [34]. The authors propose a novel framework that allows multiple participants to collaboratively train a neural network while ensuring that their training data remains confidential. This is achieved through a technique called *selective gradient sharing*, where participants only share a subset of their model updates, rather than their raw data, during the training process. These updates are further protected using DP, ensuring that the shared gradients do not reveal sensitive information about the individual data points. The framework effectively balances the trade-off between privacy and model utility, maintaining high model accuracy while providing strong privacy guarantees. The authors also address scalability by designing the system to efficiently handle many participants. Extensive experiments demonstrate that the proposed method can train deep learning models with a minimal loss in accuracy compared to standard training methods.

Rieke et al. explore the transformative potential of FL in the healthcare sector [35]. The authors highlight how FL enables the training of ML models on decentralized data, preserving patient privacy by keeping data localized on healthcare providers' servers. This approach mitigates the legal and ethical concerns associated with sharing sensitive health data. By collaborating on a global scale, healthcare institutions can leverage diverse datasets to improve model accuracy and generalizability, leading to better diagnostic tools and treatment plans.

Kaissis et al. focus on secure, privacy-preserving, and federated ML methods specifically applied to medical imaging [36]. Medical imaging datasets are often sensitive and subject to strict privacy regulations, making traditional centralized approaches challenging. FL offers a decentralized paradigm where models are trained across institutions without sharing raw data, thereby preserving patient privacy. The authors review the application of FL in medical imaging, emphasizing techniques such as DP, secure aggregation, and encryption methods tailored for healthcare settings. They discuss the benefits of FL in enabling collaborative model training across distributed datasets while complying with regulatory frameworks like GDPR and HIPAA.

Kanwal et al. address the challenge of balancing privacy concerns with the advancement of artificial intelligence in the context of histopathology for biomedical research and education [37]. Histopathological data is rich in information crucial for medical diagnostics and research but is inherently sensitive due to its potential to reveal patient identities. The authors focus on anonymization techniques aimed at safeguarding patient privacy while enabling meaningful analysis and AI model training. They review various anonymization methods applicable to histopathological images, such as pixelization, blurring, and generative models that synthesize realistic yet privacy-preserving images. The work also discusses the trade-offs between anonymization effectiveness and data utility, emphasizing the importance of preserving diagnostic accuracy and research value.

Choudhury et al. explore methods to enhance privacy in FL by anonymizing data [38]. The authors discuss various anonymization techniques, such as DP, which add noise to data to obscure individual contributions while maintaining overall utility. They also explore methods like data generalization and k-anonymity to protect identities within datasets. The work also examines the trade-offs between the degree of anonymization and the accuracy of the trained models, aiming to find a balance that maintains both privacy and model performance. Experimental results show that appropriate anonymization can significantly reduce privacy risks without severely impacting the learning outcomes.

Almashaqbeh & Ghodsi introduce AnoFel, a framework designed to support anonymity in privacy-preserving FL [39]. AnoFel addresses privacy concerns in FL by incorporating advanced anonymization techniques to enhance participant privacy without compromising the integrity and utility of the learned model. The framework employs cryptographic methods, such as HE and secure multiparty computation, to anonymize data contributions while allowing accurate aggregation. AnoFel also integrates DP to add an extra layer of protection against inference attacks. The authors present experimental results demonstrating that AnoFel effectively maintains high model accuracy while providing robust anonymity and privacy guarantees.

Zhao et al. focus on developing a framework for anonymous and privacy-preserving FL tailored to industrial big data applications [40]. The authors address the privacy risks associated with FL by proposing advanced anonymization techniques to safeguard individual data contributions. Their framework leverages DP and SMPC to ensure that data remains anonymous and protected during the aggregation process. This work highlights the unique challenges posed by industrial big data, such as the need for scalability and efficiency in handling large datasets. Experimental results demonstrate that their approach maintains high model accuracy while providing robust privacy and anonymity guarantees.

Agiollo et al. introduce a novel approach to FL called Anonymous FL via Named-Data Networking (NDN) [41]. The authors propose leveraging NDN to enhance anonymity and privacy in FL, as NDN focuses on content rather than data sources, thus naturally obfuscating the participants' identities. The proposed framework incorporates cryptographic techniques to secure data exchanges and ensure that model updates remain anonymous throughout the learning process. Experimental results demonstrate that their NDN-based approach effectively preserves privacy without compromising the efficiency and accuracy of the FL model.

Kobsa & Schreck explore the use of pseudonymity as a method for enhancing privacy in user-adaptive systems [42]. User-adaptive systems tailor their functionality and content to individual users, often requiring extensive personal data to do so. The authors argue that while such systems improve user experience, they also pose significant privacy risks. They propose pseudonymity as a solution, where users interact with the system under pseudonyms rather than their real identities. This approach allows users to benefit from personalization while minimizing the exposure of their personal information. The work also discusses various pseudonymity techniques and their effectiveness in protecting user privacy.

Gu et al. provide a comprehensive review of privacy enhancement methods for FL in healthcare systems [43]. The authors discuss the unique privacy challenges in healthcare FL, such as sensitive patient information and strict regulatory requirements like HIPAA and GDPR. They review various privacy-preserving techniques, including DP, which adds noise to data to obscure individual contributions, and HE. The work also covers secure multi-party computation, enabling multiple parties to jointly compute a function without revealing their inputs, and federated averaging algorithms designed to mitigate privacy risks.

5. Real-world applications of FL

FL (FL) is rapidly gaining traction across various industries due to its ability to leverage decentralized data while preserving privacy. This section explores the real-world applications and case studies of FL in healthcare, finance, mobile and edge devices, and highlights specific implementations like Google's Gboard and collaborative healthcare research projects.

5.1 Healthcare sector

Healthcare is one of the most promising fields for the application of FL due to the sensitive nature of medical data and the potential for improved patient outcomes through collaborative research and development.

5.1.1 Collaborative research and development

The healthcare sector stands to benefit significantly from FL due to the collaborative potential it offers while ensuring the privacy and security of sensitive medical data. This approach facilitates collaborative research and development among various healthcare institutions, leading to enhanced medical insights, improved diagnostic tool, and better patient outcomes.

FL allows multiple healthcare institutions to collaborate on research projects without sharing their data directly. This is particularly important in healthcare, where a patient data privacy is paramount, and regulations like the HIPAA and the GDPR impose strict controls on data sharing.

Medical Imaging: FL allows hospitals and medical institutions to collaboratively train models on medical imaging data (e.g., MRI and CT scans) without transferring patient data off-site. This leads to the development of more robust and accurate diagnostic tools. For example, models can be trained to detect tumors, fractures, and other anomalies more effectively by pooling data from multiple sources.

Genomic Research: Genomic data are highly sensitive and often subject to strict privacy regulations. FL enables researchers to build predictive models for genetic diseases and personalized medicine by aggregating insights from data distributed across different research centers and biobanks.

Electronic Health Records (EHRs): EHRs contain vast amounts of patient information that can be used to predict patient outcomes, optimize treatment plans, and identify potential health risks. FL facilitates the development of predictive models that can analyze EHRs from multiple hospitals without compromising patient privacy.

5.1.2 Maintaining patient privacy

Maintaining patient privacy is paramount in healthcare applications of FL due to the highly sensitive nature of medical data. FL addresses this concern by implementing several advanced techniques that ensure data privacy and security while still enabling collaborative research and model training. Here are some key approaches used to maintain patient privacy. Methods such as DP, secure multiparty computation (SMPC), HE, federated averaging, secure aggregation, and anonymization can all be useful in maintaining privacy of patient data.

SMPC and HE enable different healthcare institutions to collaboratively train a ML model without revealing their individual datasets to each other. Each participating institution encrypts its local model updates before sending them to the central server. The central server performs computations on these encrypted updates and aggregates them to improve the global model. By ensuring that raw data never leaves the local institution and remains encrypted during processing, SMPC provides a robust mechanism to protect patient privacy. DP adds random noise to the patient data or model updates from each institution before sending them to the central server. This added noise obscures individual datapoints, making it impossible to infer specific patient information from the aggregated model.

Federated Averaging (FedAvg) aggregated model updates from multiple clients (e.g., hospitals) in a privacy-preserving manner. Local models are trained on patient data within each institution. The resulting updates (model parameters) are sent to a central server, which averages these updates to form a new global model. Since only model parameters are shared and not the actual patient data, FedAvg significantly reduces the risk of data breaches and maintains patient privacy.

Anonymization removes all personal identifiable information (PII) from the data, making it impossible to link the data back to specific patients. Pseudonymization replaces personal identifiers with pseudonyms, allowing for indirect identification while still protecting patient privacy.

5.2 Financial sector

In the finance sector, FL addresses the critical need to protect sensitive financial data while improving the accuracy and robustness of models used for various applications.

5.2.1 Improving fraud detection algorithms

Fraud Detection: Fraud detection is a critical application in the financial sector. FL allows financial institutions to enhance fraud detection algorithms by training models on transaction data from multiple banks. This collaborative approach helps in identifying patterns and anomalies that might be missed when using data from a single source. The use of techniques like MPC and HE ensures that the transaction data remains private and secure.

Credit Scoring: Credit scoring models benefit from diverse data sources to improve accuracy and fairness. FL allows financial institutions to share insights without compromising privacy. Banks and financial institutions train local models on their credit data and share the updates with a central server. The aggregated model benefits from a broader dataset, leading to more accurate credit scoring. Techniques like DP ensure that individual credit data points are obfuscated, maintaining data privacy while improving model accuracy.

Anti-Money Laundering (AML): AML requires analyzing vast amounts of transaction data to identify suspicious activities. FL facilitates collaboration among financial institutions to enhance AML models. Financial institutions train local AML models on their transaction data and share encrypted updates for aggregation. The global model benefits from diverse data sources, improving its ability to detect money-laundering activities. Techniques like SAP and HE ensure that the transaction data remains confidential and secure throughout the process.

5.2.2 Ensuring data privacy

Secure Aggregation: Techniques like SAP ensure that individual financial institutions' data contributions remain confidential while still contributing to the global model.

Differential Privacy: Adding noise to the updates ensures that sensitive financial transactions cannot be traced back to individual users.

5.2.3 Case study: Bank fraud detection

Fraud detection is a critical application within the financial sector, where identifying and preventing fraudulent transactions can save institutions and customers significant amounts of money and reduce the risk of financial crimes. FL provides an innovative approach to enhancing fraud detection systems by enabling banks to collaborate without exposing sensitive transaction data. This case study explores how a consortium of banks can leverage FL for fraud detection while ensuring data privacy and security.

Background: Fraud detection involves monitoring transactions for unusual patterns that may indicate fraudulent activity, such as identity theft, unauthorized transactions, or money laundering. Traditionally, banks develop fraud detection models based on their internal data, which limits the models' effectiveness due to the lack of diverse data sources. By using FL, banks can collaboratively train more robust and accurate fraud detection models on a broader dataset.

Consortium Formation: A group of banks forms a consortium to collaboratively improve their fraud detection models. The consortium establishes a FL framework that allows them to train a global model without sharing raw transaction data. The banks forming the consortium get involved in the following activities: (i) local model training, (ii) secure model update sharing, (iii) centralized aggregation, and (iv) global model distribution. These activities are discussed briefly in the following.

Local Model Training: Each bank trains a local fraud detection model on its internal transaction data. This process involves data preparation and model training. In the data preparation step, transaction data are preprocessed to extract relevant features such as transaction amount, frequency, location, and time of day. The model training step involves the use of ML algorithms to train the fraud detection model on the prepared data. The model learns to identify patterns indicative of fraudulent activities.

Secure Model Update Sharing: Once the local models are trained, each bank computes the updates to the model parameters. These updates reflect the learned patterns and insights from the local data. To ensure privacy, the updates are encrypted using SMPC and HE techniques. While Secure Multiparty Computation (SMPC) encrypts the updates so that they can be securely combined with updates from other banks, HE allows computations on encrypted data, ensuring that the updates remain confidential during aggregation.

Centralized Aggregation: The encrypted model updates are sent to a central server, which aggregates the updates without decrypting them. The aggregation process combines the insights from all participating banks to create a global model. Techniques like SAP and DP ensure that the server can aggregate the updates without accessing individual updates so that data privacy is protected.

Global Model Distribution: The aggregated global model is distributed back to the participating banks. Each bank integrates the global model with its local system, improving its fraud detection capabilities with insights gained from the broader dataset. Several data privacy and security measures are taken at this stage. Data encryption techniques are used so that all model updates are encrypted before being shared, ensuring that sensitive transaction data is never exposed. DP is used to add noise to the updates, making it difficult to trace back any information to an individual transaction. The use of SAPs ensures that the central server can aggregate the model updates without accessing individual updates, protecting the privacy of the data.

Challenges: The use of FL brings is several benefits in financial fraud detection in banks such as (i) improved fraud detection accuracy, (ii) enhance data privacy and security, (iii) compliance with regulations, and (iv) higher resource efficiency. However, it involves several challenges as well. Some of the challenges are (i) high technical complexity, (ii) complexity in coordination among banks, and (iii) performance and scalability issues.

Technical complexity: Implementing FL involves complex cryptographic techniques and secure communication protocols. Banks need to invest in the necessary infrastructure and expertise to deploy these solutions effectively. Collaboration with technology providers and research institutions can help banks implement FL frameworks. Open-source FL platforms and libraries can also facilitate the adoption process.

Coordination complexity: Coordinating model training and update sharing among multiple banks requires effective communication and collaboration. Ensuring that all participants adhere to the same protocols and timelines can be challenging. Establishing a governance framework and clear communication channels can streamline coordination. Regular meetings and updates can ensure that all participants are aligned and progress is tracked effectively.

Performance issues: FL can introduce latency and computational overhead due to encryption and secure aggregation processes. Ensuring that the system scales efficiently with the number of participating banks is crucial. Optimizing encryption techniques and aggregation protocols can reduce latency and improve performance. Distributed computing and parallel processing can also enhance scalability.

5.3 Mobile and edge devices

FL is particularly well-suited for mobile and edge devices, enabling the training of ML models directly on devices like smartphones and IoT devices, thereby enhancing user experience while preserving privacy.

5.3.1 Enhancing user experience on mobile devices

Predicting Text Input: One of the most prominent applications of FL is in improving predictive text input on mobile devices. By training language models locally on user devices, FL allows for more personalized and accurate text predictions and autocorrect features.

Personalized Recommendations: FL can be used to train recommendation systems for apps, music videos, and other contents on mobile devices without sending user data to the cloud. This enhances user privacy while providing personalized experiences.

Health Monitoring: Wearable devices and health apps can use federated earning to improve models for health monitoring, such as detecting irregular heartbeats or predicting glucose levels, by leveraging data directly from users' devices.

5.3.2 Case study: Google's Gboard

Google's Gboard, the virtual keyboard app, is a prominent real-world example of FL in action. It demonstrates how FL can be used to improve ML models while maintaining user privacy. This case study elaborates on the implementation, benefits, and privacy measures of FL in the development of Gboard.

Background: Gboard is a widely used keyboard app that includes features like predictive text, autocorrection, and personalized suggestions. These features rely on ML models trained on user typing data to improve accuracy and user experience. However, collecting, and centralizing user data for model training poses significant privacy concerns. FL offers a solution by enabling the training of models directly on users' devices.

Implementation of FL in Gboard involves the following tasks (i) local model training on devices, (ii) model update transmission, (iii) aggregation and global model improvement, and (iv) integrating privacy and security protocols and algorithms. These tasks are briefly discussed in the following.

Local Model Training on Devices: Instead of sending user data to a central server, Gboard trains ML models directly on users' devices. This approach involves two steps, *data Collection* and *model training*. In the data collection phase, user interactions, such as typing patterns, text inputs, and corrections, are collected. These data never leave the user's device. The Gboard app includes a local model that learns from the user's typing data. The training process occurs in the background, utilizing the device's computational resources.

Model Update Transmission: Once the local model is trained on the device, the updates (i.e., changes in model parameters) are sent to Google's servers. To ensure privacy, these updates are processed securely. The model updates are encrypted before transmission to protect them from interception. Only relevant and necessary updates are transmitted, reducing the amount of data sent and further protecting privacy.

Aggregation and Global Model Improvement: The encrypted updates from many devices are aggregated on Google's servers to improve the global model. An SAP ensures that the server aggregates the model updates without being able to view individual updates. Techniques like DP are used to add noise to the updates, ensuring that individual users' data cannot be reverse-engineered. The improved global model, which now incorporates insights from many users, is distributed back to users' devices. This model update enhances the Gboard app's overall performance and accuracy.

Integration of Privacy and Security Protocols: The updates from millions of devices are averaged to improve the global model. This model ensures that the data remain on the device and only model updates are shared. Standard encryption protocols like TLS (Transport Layer Security) are used to secure data in transit. Secure Multiparty Computation (SMPC): techniques are also applied to further secure the aggregation process. DP techniques are employed to add noise to the model updates. This ensures that individual contributions are obfuscated and cannot be traced back to specific users. Federated Averaging (FedAvg) is the primary algorithm used for aggregating model updates. The updates from multiple devices are averaged to form the new global model. Since only the model updates, not the raw data, are shared, privacy is preserved. Moreover, FedAvg ensures that the aggregation process is computationally efficient, allowing the system to scale across millions of devices.

Impact: The FL approach has significantly improved the performance of Gboard's predictive text input and autocorrect features, providing a more personalized user experience while maintaining high privacy standards. However, there are some associated challenges too. These challenges are (i) higher technical complexity, (ii) increased computational overhead, and (iii) network latency and bandwidth issues.

Higher technical complexity: Implementing FL requires sophisticated algorithms and robust infrastructure to handle the encryption, transmission, and aggregation of model updates. Google has invested in developing and optimizing FL algorithms like FedAvg and SAPs to ensure efficient and secure implementation.

Increased computational overhead: Training models on users' devices can introduce computational overhead, potentially affecting device performance and battery life. The Gboard app is designed to perform training in the background, leveraging idle times and optimizing resource usage to minimize the impact on device performance.

Network latency and bandwidth issues: Transmitting model updates can incur network latency and bandwidth usage, especially with a large user base. Sparse and selective update transmission helps reduce the amount of data sent. Additionally, updates are often transmitted during periods of low network activity to minimize impact on user experience.

FL offers a revolutionary approach to ML by enabling collaborative model training across decentralized data sources while preserving privacy. Its application in healthcare, finance, and mobile and edge devices demonstrate the broad potential and versatility of this technology.

In healthcare, FL facilitates collaborative research and development, leading to improved diagnostic tools and personalized medicine while maintaining patient privacy. The finance sector benefits from enhanced fraud detection algorithms and credit scoring models that leverage data from multiple institutions without sharing sensitive information. Mobile and edge devices use FL to enhance user experience by training models locally, thereby preserving user privacy and providing personalized services.

Case studies like Google's Gboard and collaborative healthcare research projects illustrate the practical implementation and impact of FL. Google's Gboard demonstrates how FL can improve predictive text input on millions of devices while maintaining high privacy standards. Collaborative healthcare projects highlight the potential for FL to advance medical research and diagnostics through secure, decentralized data collaboration.

As FL continues to evolve, ongoing research and development in privacy-preserving techniques, secure aggregation, and efficient communication protocols will be crucial. By addressing the challenges and leveraging the advantages of FL, industries can harness the power of decentralized data to drive innovation, improve services, and protect user privacy.

6. Conclusion and future work

FL represents a significant advancement in the field of machine learning by addressing the crucial challenge of data privacy. This approach enables multiple entities to collaboratively train models without sharing their underlying data, thus enhancing privacy and security while maintaining model performance. Throughout this chapter, we explored the fundamentals of FL, its architecture, and workflow, and highlighted key privacy-preserving techniques such as differential privacy, encryption, and secure aggregation. Additionally, we examined the practical applications of FL in various sectors including healthcare, finance, mobile and edge devices, and industrial IoT.

The architecture of FL involves a central server and multiple local clients. The central server coordinates the overall training process, initializes model parameters, aggregates model updates, and manages communication with clients. Local clients retain their data, perform local training, compute model updates, and transmit these updates to the central server. This decentralized approach ensures that sensitive data remains localized, mitigating privacy risks associated with traditional centralized models.

Key privacy-preserving techniques discussed include differential privacy, which introduces noise to model updates to protect individual data points, and secure aggregation, which ensures that individual contributions remain confidential during the aggregation process. These methods provide robust privacy guarantees while allowing for effective collaborative training.

As FL continues to evolve, several areas require further research and development to address existing challenges and enhance its capabilities:

Enhanced Privacy-Preserving Techniques: Developing more robust privacy-preserving mechanisms such as advanced differential privacy techniques, homomorphic encryption, and secure multi-party computation to ensure stronger privacy guarantees.

Improved Scalability: Creating scalable algorithms and infrastructure to handle the massive scale and diversity of devices in cross-device FL. This includes optimizing communication protocols and reducing the computational burden on resource-constrained devices [44].

Efficient Model Aggregation: Innovating aggregation methods that can handle the heterogeneity of updates and improve the convergence rates of global models. Techniques like federated optimization and adaptive aggregation can play a significant role.

Personalized Federated Learning (FL): Developing techniques that customize the global model for each client, boosting performance in varied and heterogeneous environments. Approaches like federated meta-learning and multi-task learning are potential areas to explore.

Robustness and Security: Enhancing the robustness of FL systems against adversarial attacks and ensuring the security of model updates. Techniques like adversarial training and secure aggregation protocols are critical [45].

Regulatory Compliance: Ensuring that FL frameworks adhere to data protection regulations across different regions. This involves continuous monitoring and updating of compliance strategies as regulations evolve.

Interdisciplinary Collaboration: Encouraging collaboration between researchers from different fields such as machine learning, cryptography, and data privacy to develop innovative solutions for FL.

By addressing the challenges mentioned above and fostering interdisciplinary collaboration, FL can continue to advance as a cornerstone of privacy-preserving machine learning. It has the potential to transform the way we approach machine learning in a privacy-conscious world, balancing the need for data-driven insights with the necessity to protect individual privacy.

Acknowledgements

The authors acknowledge the use of the AI tool ChatGPT for language polishing in some portions of the chapter.

Author details

Jaydip Sen*, Hetvi Waghela and Sneha Rakshit
Department of Data Science, Praxis Business School, Kolkata, India

*Address all correspondence to: jaydip.sen@acm.org

References

[1] Sen J. Homomorphic encryption–theory and application. In: Sen J, editor. Theory and Practice of Cryptography and Network Security Protocols and Technologies. London, UK: InTechOpen; 2011. pp. 1-30. DOI: 10.5772/56687

[2] Sen J, Maitra S. An attack on privacy preserving data aggregation protocol for wireless sensor networks. In: Laud P, editor. Proceedings of the 16th Nordic Conference in Secure IT Systems (NordSec 2011), Tallinn Estonia, LNCS. Vol. 7161. Heidelberg, Germany: Springer; 2011. pp. 205-222. DOI: 10.1007/978-3-642-29615-4_15

[3] Qammar A, Karim A, Ning H, Ding J. Securing federated learning with blockchain: A systematic literature review. Artificial Intelligence Review. 2023;**56**:3951-3985. DOI: 10.1007/s10462-022-10271-9

[4] McMahan HB, Ramage D, Talwar K, Zhang L. Learning differentially private recurrent language model. In: Proceedings of ICLR 2018. Vancouver, Canada; April 30 - May 3 2018. DOI: 10.48550/arXiv.1710.06963

[5] Abadi M, Chu A, Goodfellow I, McMahan HB, Mironov I, Talwar K, et al. Deep learning with differential privacy. In: Proceedings of the ACM SIGSAC Conference on Computer and Communications Security. Vienna, Austria; 24-28 October 2016. pp. 308-318. DOI: 10.1145/2976749.2978318

[6] Geyer RC, Klein T, Nabi M. Differentially private FL: A client level perspective. In: Proceedings of NIPS Workshop on ML on the Phone and Other Consumer Devices. Long Beach, CA, USA; 4-9 December 2017. DOI: 10.48550/arXiv.1712.07557

[7] Fu J, Hong Y, Ling X, Wang L, Ran X, Sun Z, et al. Differentially private FL: A systematic review. arXiv. 2024;**arXiv**:2405.08299

[8] Gu X, Zhu T, Li J, Zhang T, Ren W. The impact of differential privacy on model fairness in FL. In: Kutyłowski M, Zhang J, Chen C, editors. Network and System Security. NSS 2020, Lecture Notes in Computer Science. Vol. 12570. Cham: Springer; 2020. pp. 419-430. DOI: 10.1007/978-3-030-65745-1_25

[9] Li Y, Xu J, Zhu J, Wang X. An optimized scheme of FL based on differential privacy. In: Chen J, Wen B, Chen T, editors. Blockchain and Trustworthy Systems. BlockSys, Communications in Computer and Information Science. Vol. 1896. Singapore: Springer; 2023. pp. 285-295. DOI: 10.1007/978-981-99-8101-4_20

[10] Löbner S, Gogov B, Tesfay WB. Enhancing privacy in FL with local differential privacy for email classification. In: Garcia-Alfaro J, Navarro-Arribas G, Dragoni N, editors. Data Privacy Management, Cryptocurrencies and Blockchain Technology. DPM CBT 2022, Lecture Notes in Computer Science. Vol. 13619. Cham: Springer; 2022. pp. 3-18. DOI: 10.1007/978-3-031-25734-6_1

[11] Wei K, Li J, Ding M, Ma C, Yang HH, Farhad F, et al. FL with differential privacy: Algorithms and performance analysis. Vol. 15. IEEE Transactions on Information Forensics and Security. 2020. pp. 3454-3469. DOI: 10.1109/TIFS.2020.2988575

[12] Li M, Tian Y, Feng Y, Yu Y. Federated transfer learning with differential privacy. arXiv. 2024;**arXiv**:2403.11343

[13] Park S, Choi W. On the differential privacy in FL based on over-the-air computation. IEEE Transaction on Wireless Communications. 2024;**23**(5):4269-4283. DOI: 10.1109/TWC.2023.3316788

[14] Bonawitz P, Ivanov V, Kreuter B, Marcedone A, McMahan HB, Patel S, et al. Practical secure aggregation for FL on user-held data. In: Proceedings of NIPS Workshop on Private Multi-Party ML. Barcelona, Spain; 9 December 2016

[15] Truex S, Baracaldo N, Anwar A, Steinke T, Ludwig H, Zhang R, et al. A hybrid approach to privacy-preserving FL. In: Proceedings of the 12th ACM Workshop on Artificial Intelligence and Security. London, United Kingdom; 15 November 2019. pp. 1-11. DOI: 10.1145/3338501.3357370

[16] Phong LT, Aono Y, Hayashi T, Wang L, Moriai S. Privacy-preserving deep learning: Revisited and enhanced. In: Batten L, Kim D, Zhang X, Li G, editors. Applications and Techniques in Information Security, ATIS 2017, Communications in Computer and Information Science. Vol. 719. Singapore: Springer; 2017. pp. 100-110. DOI: 10.1007/978-981-10-5421-1_9

[17] Park J, Lim H. Privacy-preserving FL using HE. Applied Sciences. 2022;**12**(2):734. DOI: 10.3390/app12020734

[18] Kurniawan H, Mambo M. HE-based federated privacy preservation for deep active learning. Entropy. 2022;**24**:1545. DOI: 10.3390/e24111545

[19] Nguyen T, Thai MT. Preserving privacy and security in FL. IEEE/ACM Transactions on Networking. 2023;**32**(1):833-843. DOI: 10.1109/TNET.2023.330201

[20] Gao Y, Zhang L, Wang L, Choo K-KR, Zhang R. Privacy-preserving and reliable decentralized FL. IEEE Transactions on Services Computing. 2023;**16**(4):2879-2891. DOI: 10.1109/TSC.2023.3250705

[21] Mothukuri V, Parizi RM, Pouriyeh S, Huang Y, Dehghantanha A, Srivastava G. A survey on security and privacy of FL. Future Generation Computer System. 2021;**115**:619-640. DOI: 10.1016/j.future.2020.10.007

[22] Zhao J, Zhu H, Wang F, Zheng Y, Liu R, Li H. Efficient and privacy-preserving FL against poisoning adversaries. IEEE Transactions on Services Computing. 2024. DOI: 10.1109/TSC.2024.3377931

[23] Wang Y, Zhang A, Wu S, Yu S. VOSA: Verifiable and oblivious secure aggregation for privacy-preserving FL. IEEE Transactions on Dependable and Secure Computing. 2023;**20**(5):3601-3616. DOI: 10.1109/TDSC.2022.3226508

[24] Zhao L, Jiang J, Feng B, Wang Q, Shen C, Li Q. SEAR: Secure and efficient aggregation for byzantine-robust FL. IEEE Transactions on Dependable and Secure Computing. 2022;**19**(5):3329-3342. DOI: 10.1109/TDSC.2021.3093711

[25] So J, Guler B, Avestimehr AS. Turbo-aggregate: Breaking the quadratic aggregation barrier in secure FL. arXiv. 2020;**arXiv**:2002.04156

[26] Rathee M, Shen C, Wagh S, Popa RA. ELSA: Secure aggregation for FL with malicious actors. In: Proceedings of the IEEE Symposium on Security and Privacy (SP). San Francisco, CA, USA; 21-25 May 2023. pp. 1961-1979. DOI: 10.1109/SP46215.2023.10179468

[27] Fereidooni H et al. SAFELearn: Secure aggregation for private

FL. In: Proceedings of the IEEE Security and Privacy Workshops (SPW). San Francisco, CA, USA; May 2021. pp. 56-62. DOI: 10.1109/SPW53761.2021.00017

[28] Zhong Y, Tan W, Xu Z, Chen S, Weng J, Weng J. WVFL: Weighted verifiable secure aggregation in FL. IEEE Internet of Things Journal. 2024;**11**(11):19926-19936. DOI: 10.1109/JIOT.2024.3370938

[29] Zhou S, Lio M, Qiao B, Yang X. A survey of security aggregation. In: Proceedings of the 24th International Conference on Advanced Communication Technology. PyeongChang Kwangwoon_Do, Korea, Republic of, February 13-16. 2022. pp. 334-340. DOI: 10.23919/ICACT53585.2022.9728912

[30] Sami HU, Güler B. Secure aggregation for clustered federated learning. In: Proceedings of IEEE International Symposium on Information Theory (ISIT). Taipei, Taiwan, USA: IEEE; 15-30 June 2023. pp. 186-191. DOI: 10.1109/ISIT54713.2023.10206964

[31] Liu Y, Qian X, Li H, Hao M, Guo S. Fast secure aggregation for privacy-preserving FL. In: Proceedings of IEEE Global Comm Conference. Rio de Janeiro, Brazil, USA: IEEE; 4-8 December 2022. pp. 3017-3022. DOI: 10.1109/GLOBECOM48099.2022.10001327

[32] Truong N, Sun K, Wang S, Guitton F, Guo Y. Privacy preservation in FL: An insightful survey form the GDPR perspective. Computers & Security. 2021;**110**:102402. DOI: 10.1016/j.cose.2021.102402

[33] Li H, Ge L, Tian L. Survey: FL data security and privacy-preserving in edge-internet of things. Artificial Intelligence Review. 2024;**57**:130. DOI: 10.1007/s10462-024-10774-7

[34] Shokri R, Shmatikov V. Privacy-preserving deep learning. In: Proceedings of the 53rd Annual Allerton Conference on Communications, Control, and Computing (Allerton). Monticello, IL, USA; September 29 - October 2 2015. pp. 909-910. DOI: 10.1109/ALLERTON.2015.7447103

[35] Rieke N, Hancox J, Li W, et al. The future of digital health with FL. npj Digital Medicine. 2020;**3**:119. DOI: 10.1038/s41746-020-00323-1

[36] Kaissis GA, Makowski MR, Rückert D, Braren RF. Secure, privacy-preserving and federated ML in medical imaging. Nature Machine Intelligence. 2020;**2**:305-311. DOI: 10.1038/s42256-020-0186-1

[37] Kanwal N, Janssen EAM, Engan K. Balancing Privacy and Progress in Artificial Intelligence: Anonymization in Histopathology for Biomedical Research and Education. In: Farmanbar M, Tzamtzi M, Verma AK. Chakravorty A editors. Frontiers of Artificial Intelligence, Ethics, and Multidisciplinary Applications. FAIEMA 2023. Springer: Singapore; 2024. pp. 417-429. DOI: 10.1007/978-981-99-9836-4_31

[38] Choudhury O, Gkoulalas-Divanis A, Salonidis T, Sylla I, Park Y, Hsu G, et al. Anonymizing data for privacy-preserving FL. In: Proceedings of the 24th European Conference on Artificial Intelligence (ECAI'20), Santiago de Compostela, Spain. August 29-September 8 2020

[39] Almashaqbeh G, Ghodsi Z. AnoFel: Supporting anonymity for privacy-preserving FL. arXiv. 2023;**arXiv**:2306.06825

[40] Zhao B, Fan K, Yang K, Wang Z, Li H, Yang Y. Anonymous and privacy-preserving FL with industrial big data. IEEE Transactions on Industrial Informatics. 2021;**17**(9):6314-6323. DOI: 10.1109/TII.2021.3052183

[41] Agiollo A, Bardhi E, Conti M, Fabbro ND, Lazzeretti R. Anonymous FL via named-data networking. Future Generation Computer Systems. 2024;**152**:288-303. DOI: 10.1016/j.future.2023.11.009

[42] Kobsa A, Schreck J. Privacy through pseudonymity in user-adaptive systems. ACM Transactions on Internet Technology. 2003;**3**(2):149-183. DOI: 10.1145/767193.767196

[43] Gu X, Sabrina F, Fan Z, Sohail S. A review of privacy enhancement methods for FL in healthcare systems. International Journal of Environmental Research, MDPI. 2023;**20**(15):1-25. DOI: 10.3390/ijerph20156539

[44] Sen J, Dasgupta S. Data privacy preservation on the internet of things. In: Sen J, Mayer J, editors. Information Security and Privacy in the Digital World: Some Selected Topics. London, UK: IntechOpen; 2023. ISBN: 978-1-83768-196-9

[45] Sen J. A survey of cryptography and key management schemes for wireless sensor networks. In: Sen J, Yi M, Niu F, Wu H, editors. Wireless Sensor Networks: Research Issues and Effective Smart Solutions. London, UK: IntechOpen; 2023. DOI: 10.5772/intechopen.112277

Chapter 3

Privacy-Preserving Algorithms in Distributed Optimization Problems

Lingying Huang, Rong Su, Xiaomeng Chen and Junfeng Wu

Abstract

With the rise in computational complexity and network scale, distributed optimization problems have gained increasing interest due to their robustness and scalability advantages over centralized approaches. It has been widely applied in various scenarios. However, privacy concerns can deter participants from sharing their sensitive data in such networks. To address this issue, we introduce methods to preserve privacy in distributed optimization problems, particularly over unbalanced directed communication networks, in this chapter. Two algorithms, namely, PP-DOAGT and SD-Push-Pull, are introduced in detail to balance the tradeoff between performance and privacy. PP-DOAGT ensures privacy over infinite iterations and highlights two fundamental impossibility results concerning privacy and performance. Due to the second dilemma, the tradeoff between ε-DP and performance analysis is studied under summable stepsize sequences in PP-DOAGT. In contrast, SD-Push-Pull focuses on guaranteeing privacy over finite iterations. Through state decomposition, this algorithm attains linear convergence with an unchanged stepsize, approaching neighborhood of optimum under certain conditions. With the proposed methods, privacy can be guaranteed in real application scenarios such as machine learning, allowing participants to confidently share their data within distributed optimization frameworks.

Keywords: privacy-preserving, distributed optimization problems, directed communication networks, tradeoff between privacy and performance, machine learning application

1. Introduction

Distributed optimization has been widely applied to a wide application scenario, especially for large-scale networks [1–6]. Estrin *et al.* [7] showed that distributed optimization offers greater robustness and scalability advantages compared to centralized ones. Various studies have proposed different kind of distributed optimization algorithms to collaboratively solve problems by sharing information with neighbors.

Extensive research has been conducted on distributed optimization through undirected communication networks, as seen in works by Nedic and Ozdagalar [8], Ram *et al.* [9], Duchi *et al.* [10], and Shi *et al.* [11]. These studies typically rely on doubly stochastic mixing matrices. However, for directed graphs (digraphs), which include undirected graphs as a special case, the doubly stochastic matrix assumption generally does not hold. To address this, [12, 13] introduced push-sum-based distributed optimization algorithms for digraphs. However, this kind of algorithm has a drawback since it cannot guarantee that the available stepsize set for convergence is nonempty. The interval is further relaxed by Xi *et al.* [14] while maintaining linear convergence. In the meanwhile, the algorithms in above literature need extra communication and computation cost to address the imbalance problem. To tackle this, AB/Push-Pull, which tracks the state along with the function's gradient was introduced by the authors in Refs. [15, 16], eliminating extra burden for eigenvector learning. In contrast to the push-sum protocol, this kind of algorithm uses two stochastic mix matrices, in which allows the agent to choose the weight by their local knowledge, providing flexibility in network design and unifying various communication architectures. Pu The robustness is further considered in [17], allowing for quick adaptation to agent extraction and noise influence.

The gradient-tracking algorithms mentioned above, despite differences in implementation, share a common feature: each participant will hold and exchange two variables, one to track the best decision while the other to track the estimates of a function of the gradient set. This makes the exchanged data unprotected and accessible by malicious attackers, leading to the potential disclosure of confidential information and serious disasters, such as the malicious use of personal data and even economic losses of the country [18]. The urgent need to obtain optimal solutions distributively while safeguarding critical information has led to significant research efforts. Dwork *et al.* [19] (see [20] for a survey) first introduced the concept of ε-differential privacy (DP). Building on this, Huang *et al.* [21] developed a DP consensus algorithm by incorporating independent, exponentially decaying Laplace noise. They extended the ε-DP concept to distributed optimization problems, proposing a new DP distributed optimization algorithm in [22]. Ding *et al.* [23, 24] further extended the algorithm to use a constant stepsize and relaxed the assumption of bounded gradients. However, these works focused on undirected graphs, making extension to directed communication network topologies challenging because of the requirement of doubly stochastic matrices.

For most practical applications, information flows among sensors may be unidirectional because of different communication ranges, as seen in coordinated vehicle control problems [25] and economic dispatch problems [26]. To mitigate privacy leakage for nodes communicating through unbalanced digraphs, an algorithm utilizing the gradient-tracking approach with a diminishing stepsize that preserves the privacy is developed by Mao *et al.* [27]. This algorithm was demonstrated through an example of an economic dispatch problem. Despite its effectiveness, the algorithm did not include a formal privacy definition and fell short of obtaining DP. The weight-balancing method is adopted by Zhu *et al.* [28] to address asymmetry. Nevertheless, this method requires the knowledge of each node's out-degree, which is difficult to obtain in some scenarios, especially broadcast systems. Xiong *et al.* [29] provided a push-sum-based privacy-preserving algorithm, where the weights are balanced by introducing an auxiliary variable. However, the push-sum protocol has inherent shortcomings, including reliance on a decaying stepsize for convergence and stricter communication topology requirements. In contrast, gradient-tracking algorithms have fewer stepsize requirements compared with the studies [15, 16]. Gao *et al.* [30] allowed each agent to randomly decide the mixing matrices to preserve privacy since the gradient variables will become indistinguishable. However, if adversaries know the coupling weights, the algorithm cannot preserve privacy of the sensitive gradient information. Wang [31] introduced a novel gradient-tracking-based method that prevents the buildup of noise from information sharing in gradient estimates, ensuring almost sure convergence of each agent to the optimum. A limitation of this approach is the requirement of the left eigenvector of the communication graph at each iteration, which is generally global information. To sum up, the tradeoff between performance and privacy has not been thoroughly investigated, particularly for directed topologies.

In this chapter, methods to preserve privacy in distributed optimization problems via directed network topologies are introduced in Section 2. The tradeoff between privacy and performance considering different methods is analyzed in Section 3. The application scenarios are included in Section 4 while conclusions are summarized in Section 5.

2. Methods to preserve privacy in distributed optimization problems

In recent years, studies on privacy preservation have been categorized into four main approaches: anonymity, cryptography, perturbation, and state decomposition.

1. Anonymity aims to protect the identification of participants [32]. However, designing effective anonymity methods often requires background information about the system, which is challenging to obtain without a centralized and trusted server [33].

2. Cryptography is the most direct and commonly used method for preserving privacy, as demonstrated in recent works [34, 35]. Despite its effectiveness, it incurs high computational and communication costs.

3. Perturbation, particularly DP, introduces randomness into the original data. This method ensures that outputs remain similar even when inputs differ by a single entry, providing provable privacy guarantees independent of the eavesdropper's computational power, as demonstrated in recent works [21–24, 28]. However, a balance must always be struck between privacy and performance.

4. State decomposition is a unique method for preserving privacy in multi-agent systems, first proposed by Wang [36]. The key concept involves dividing a node's original state into two substates: a visible state that is communicated between neighbors and a hidden state that is accessible only to the originating node.

From the above analysis, the first two methods are not suitable for distributed optimization problems. Anonymity requires a centralized trusted server, which contradicts the decentralized nature of distributed systems. Cryptography, while effective, imposes significant computational and communication costs on distributed nodes, negating the advantages of distributed optimization. Therefore, we will focus on the last two methods for distributed optimization problems in the following discussion.

2.1 Distributed optimization problems via directed network topologies

The considered system consists N agents (nodes) that communicate via a digraph, solving the following problem collaboratively:

$$\min_{x \in \mathbb{R}^m} \sum_{i=1}^{N} f_i(x). \tag{1}$$

Here, x represents a global decision variable, while $f_i : \mathbb{R}^m \to \mathbb{R}$ is a convex function known exclusively by each node i.

In addition, a digraph $G = (\mathcal{N}, \mathcal{E})$ is utilized to model the interaction topology, where $\mathcal{N} = \{1, 2, \dots, N\}$ denotes the set of node indices, and $\mathcal{E} \subset \mathcal{N} \times \mathcal{N}$ indicates the set of communication links. In G, a directed edge $(j, i) \in \mathcal{E}$ signifies a presence of a directional communication link from agent j to agent i. Furthermore, a directed tree refers to a directed graph where each node expect for the root node. Moreover, a spanning tree of a directed graph [37] is a directed tree linking the root to all other nodes in the graph. A digraph $G_M = (\mathcal{N}, \mathcal{E}_M)$ is described by a nonnegative matrix $M = [M_{ij}] \in \mathbb{R}^{N \times N}$ where an edge $(j, i) \in \mathcal{E}_M$ exists if $Mij > 0$. The in-neighbor and out-neighbor sets of node i are respectively given by

$$\mathcal{N}_{M,i}^{\text{in}} = \{j : (j, i) \in \mathcal{E}_M\} \text{ and } \mathcal{N}_{M,i}^{\text{out}} = \{j : (i, j) \in \mathcal{E}_M\}. \tag{2}$$

To solve the optimization problem distributively, each agent i holds a local decision variable $x_i \in \mathbb{R}^m$. Thus, Problem (1) is reformulated as

$$\begin{aligned} \mathfrak{P} : \min_{x_1, x_2, \dots, x_N \in \mathbb{R}^m} & \sum_{i=1}^{N} f_i(x_i) \\ \text{s.t.} x_1 = x_2 = & \dots = x_N. \end{aligned} \tag{3}$$

Here, we add the requirement of achieving the same decision variable among different agents as a constraint.

To make $\mathfrak{P}$ have a unique solution, we assume the required function sets satisfy the following assumption.

Assumption 1. The local function of each agent i, i.e., f_i, is μ-strongly convex and L-smooth with $\mu \leq L$.

Under Assumption 1, let $x^* \in \mathbb{R}^m$ denote the unique solution to $\mathfrak{P}$, where $\sum_{i=1}^{N} \nabla f_i(x^*) = 0$.

For convenience, we characterize the distributed optimization problem $\mathfrak{P}$ by $(\mathcal{X}, \mathcal{F}, f, G)$ [22]:

1. *Domain*: the domain of optimization is denoted as $\mathcal{X} = \mathbb{R}^m$;

2. *Function set and collaborative function*: the collection of real-valued, strongly convex, and differentiable individual cost functions is denoted as $\mathcal{F} \subseteq \mathcal{X} \to \mathbb{R}$. The overall collaborative function is expressed as $f(x) = \sum_{i=1}^{N} f_i(x)$, where $f_i \in \mathcal{F}$;

3. *Communication topology*: the communication topology is represented by G.

There are various methods to solve $\mathfrak{P}$ distributively. In this chapter, we deal with distributed algorithms where both estimate of the optimum $x_i(k) \in \mathbb{R}^m$ and estimate of the collaborative function gradient $y_i(k) \in \mathbb{R}^m$ are maintained and updated by node i following:

$$
\begin{aligned}
y_i(k+1) &= (1-\gamma)y_i(k) + \gamma \sum_{j=0}^{N} C_{ij} y_j(k) + \alpha_k \nabla f_i(x_i(k)) \\
x_i(k+1) &= (1-\varpi)x_i(k) + \varpi \sum_{j=0}^{N} R_{ij} x_j(k) - y_i(k+1) + y_i(k),
\end{aligned}
\tag{4}
$$

where the estimate of decision variable and collaborative function gradient $x_i(0)$ and $y_i(0)$, $\forall i \in \mathcal{N}$ can be any initializations, and $\gamma, \varpi \in (0, 1]$. This kind of algorithms is called as DOAGT [38]. This kind of algorithm allows each node i to decide the in-graph G_R and out-graph $\mathrm{G}_{C^\top}$ locally satisfying Assumption 2.

Assumption 2. The weight matrices corresponding to G_R and $\mathrm{G}_{C^\top}$ satisfy:

1. R and C are nonnegative weight matrix where $R\mathbf{1} = \mathbf{1}$ and $\mathbf{1}^\top C = \mathbf{1}^\top$;

2. $R_{ij} > 0$ only for the in-neighbors of node i, otherwise, $R_{ij} = 0$;

3. $C_{li} > 0$ only for the out-neighbors of node i, otherwise, $C_{li} = 0$.

To ensure that (4) eventually converges with a carefully chosen stepsize, the following assumption regarding the graph connectivity is introduced.

Assumption 3. The induced graphs G_R and $\mathrm{G}_{C^\top}$ each include at least one spanning tree, respectively. In addition, there is at least one node that serves as the root of spanning trees in both G_R and $\mathrm{G}_{C^\top}$.

This assumption offers greater flexibility in selecting the graph topology compared to other distributed algorithms referenced in [14, 15, 39, 40], necessitating both the communication topology G_R and $\mathrm{G}_{C^\top}$ to be strongly connected.

2.2 DP in distributed optimization problems

DP is a concept that quantifies the degree of privacy protection for individuals within a statistical database. In the first place, we provide the necessary background by presenting the subsequent definitions as preliminaries for understanding DP in the context of distributed optimization.

Different from other paper, we characterize δ-adjacency of two distributed optimization problems based on the following definition.

Definition 1 (δ-adjacency) If the following requirements are met, we call the two distributed optimization problems $\mathfrak{P}$ and $\mathfrak{P}'$ are δ-adjacent:

1. $\mathcal{X} = \mathcal{X}'$, $\mathcal{F} = \mathcal{F}'$, and $\mathrm{G} = \mathrm{G}'$, that is, the domain, the function set, together with the communication topology are all the same;

2. there is an $i_0 \in \mathcal{N}$ with different function, i.e.,$f_{i_0} \neq f'_{i_0}$ and for all other functions are identical, i.e., $j \neq i_0 \in \mathcal{N}, f_j = f'_j$;

3. the distance of the different gradient functions, i.e., ∇f_{i_0} and $\nabla f'_{i_0}$, is bounded by δ across the whole domain $\mathcal{X}$, i.e., $\sup_{x \in \mathcal{X}} \|\nabla f_{i_0}(x) - \nabla f'_{i_0}(x)\|_1 \leq \delta$.

According to the above definition, if the two distributed optimization problems vary only in the cost function of one node, with all other conditions remaining unchanged, they are deemed δ-adjacent. This concept of δ-adjacency ralexes the requirement in [22], which mandates bounded gradients on the domain of optimization. If we assume $\|\nabla f_i(x)\|_1 \leq c, \forall i \in \mathcal{N}$ as in [22], setting $\delta = 2c$ ensures $\|\nabla f_{i_0}(x) - \nabla f'_{i_0}(x)\|_1 \leq \|\nabla f_{i_0}(x)\|_1 + \|\nabla f'_{i_0}(x)\|_1 \leq \delta$. In addition, $\delta-$adjacency accommodates a broader range of function sets. For example, $f_{i_0}(x) = x^\top Qx$ and $f'_{i_0}(x) = x^\top Qx + p^\top x$ with $\|p\|_1 \leq \delta$ and $Q > 0$ with the domain $x \in \mathbb{R}^m$ are only δ-adjacent in our definition.

Under DOAGT (4), we consider the worst case that the eavesdropper can access as much informaiton as they can, to be specific, initial state $s_0 = \{x_i(0), y_i(0)\}_{i=1}^N$, the stepsize sequence $\{\alpha_k\}_{k\in\mathbb{N}}$, the communication graph G_R, $\mathrm{G}_{C^\top}$, and algorithm parameter ϖ, γ. Other eavesdropper has less information set would have better privacy guarantee. In the worst case, transmitting $x_j(k)$ and $C_{ij}y_j(k)$ directly reveals the sensitive information since the gradient and decision value can be inferred via the following formula:

$$
\begin{aligned}
\nabla f_i(x_i(k)) &= \frac{1}{\alpha_k}\left(y_i(k+1) - \sum_{j=1}^N C'_{ij}y_j(k)\right) = \frac{1}{\alpha_k}\left(\sum_{l=1}^N C'_{li}y_i(k+1) - \sum_{j=1}^N C'_{ij}y_j(k)\right), \\
x_i(k+1) &= \sum_{j=1}^N R'_{ij}x_j(k) - \sum_{l=1}^N C'_{li}y_i(k+1) + \sum_{l=1}^N C'_{li}y_i(k),
\end{aligned} \tag{5}
$$

where R'_{ij} and, C'_{ij} are elements of the modified weighted matrix R_ϖ and C_γ with $R_\varpi = (1-\varpi)I + \varpi R = \left[R'_{ij}\right]$ and $C_\gamma = (1-\gamma)I + \gamma C = \left[C'_{ij}\right]$.

Therefore, it is essential to blur the transmitted messages by, for example, adding random noises to preserve the gradient information. Algorithm 1 (PP-DOAGT) encapsulates the resulting randomized mechanism.

Algorithm 1. PP-DOAGT [38].

Input: Stepsize sequence $\{\alpha_k\}_{k\in\mathbb{N}}$ with $\alpha_k > 0$, communication topology related parameters R, C, ϖ, γ, and initial state s_0.
Step 1: Node i initializes its states with $x_i(0)$ and $y_i(0)$, $\forall i \in \mathcal{N}$.
Step 2: At each iteration k, $\forall k \in \mathbb{N}$, $\forall i \in \mathcal{N}$:

1. Node i randomly generates the noises $\zeta_i(k), \eta_i(k) \in \mathbb{R}^m$ following certain distributions.
2. Node i pushes $C_{li}(y_i(k) + \eta_i(k))$ to $l \in \mathcal{N}_{C,i}^{\text{out}}$.
3. Node i pulls $x_j(k) + \zeta_j(k)$ from $j \in \mathcal{N}_{R,i}^{\text{in}}$.
4. After receiving $x_j(k) + \zeta_j(k)$ and $C_{ij}\left(y_j(k) + \eta_j(k)\right)$, node i updates y_i and x_i following:

$$
\begin{aligned}
y_i(k+1) = &\quad (1-\gamma)y_i(k) + \gamma\sum_j C_{ij}\left(y_j(k) + \eta_j(k)\right) + \alpha_k \nabla f_i(x_i(k)), \\
x_i(k+1) = &\quad (1-\varpi)x_i(k) + \varpi\sum_j R_{ij}\left(x_j(k) + \zeta_j(k)\right) - y_i(k+1) + y_i(k).
\end{aligned} \tag{6}
$$

We refer to $\eta_i(k)$ as the gradient-tracking noise and $\zeta_i(k)$ as the coordination noise, respectively. Stack $\eta(k) = [\eta_1(k), \ldots, \eta_N(k)]^\top \in \mathbb{R}^{N\times m}$ and $\zeta(k) = [\zeta_1(k), \ldots, \zeta_N(k)]^\top \in \mathbb{R}^{N\times m}$. A sample space $\Omega = \left(\mathbb{R}^{N\times m}\right)^{\mathbb{N}}$ denotes the set of avaiable choice of $\mathcal{W} = \{\zeta(k), \eta(k)\}_{k\in\mathbb{N}}$. Additionally, stack the state variables $x(k)$ and $y(k)$ in a similar way, i.e., $x(k) = [x_1(k), \ldots, x_N(k)]^\top \in \mathbb{R}^{N\times m}$ and $y(k) = [y_1(k), \ldots, y_N(k)]^\top \in \mathbb{R}^{N\times m}$. Lastly, denote $\nabla f(x(k)) = [\nabla f_1(x_1(k)), \ldots, \nabla f_N(x_N(k))]^\top \in \mathbb{R}^{N\times m}$. By the above definitions, the matrix form of (6) is:

$$\begin{aligned} y(k+1) &= (1-\gamma)y(k) + \gamma C y_o(k) + \alpha_k \nabla f(x(k)), \\ x(k+1) &= (1-\varpi)x(k) + \varpi R x_o(k) - y(k+1) + y(k), \\ x_o(k) &= x(k) + \zeta(k), \\ y_o(k) &= y(k) + \eta(k). \end{aligned} \tag{7}$$

For a particular problem $\mathfrak{P}$, it is obvious from (7) that the available set of output sequences, i.e., $\mathcal{O} = \{x_o(k), y_o(k)\}_{k\in\mathbb{N}}$, is uniquely determined by $\mathcal{W}$, given $\{\alpha_k\}_{k\in\mathbb{N}}$, R, C, ϖ, γ and s_0 under PP-DOAGT. Define this noise-to-output mapping $\Theta_{\mathfrak{P}} : \Omega \mapsto \Omega$. This mappings is a bijection from Ω to itself under Assumption 1 [38]. From the above analysis, the ε-DP of PP-DOAGT is defined as follows.

Definition 2 (ε-DP) For a given $\varepsilon > 0$, if for any two δ−adjacent distributed optimization problem $\mathfrak{P}$ and $\mathfrak{P}'$, any Borel set of the output sequences $\mathbb{O} \in \mathscr{B}\left(\left(\mathbb{R}^{N\times m}\right)^{\mathbb{N}}\right)$ has

$$\mathbf{P}\left[\Theta_{\mathfrak{P}}^{-1}(\mathbb{O})\right] \le e^{\varepsilon} \mathbf{P}\left[\Theta_{\mathfrak{P}'}^{-1}(\mathbb{O})\right], \tag{8}$$

we call a PP-DOAGT under Assumption 1 is ε-DP.

In essence, Definition 2 suggests that for any two similar distributed optimization problems, the distributions of the transmitted outputs are indistinguishable to an extent that prevents an adversary from identifying each individual's correct local cost function from the whole function set $\mathscr{F}$. In (8), the quantity ε represents the privacy level. If ε is smaller, it means that the two distributions are more indistinguishable; thus, the privacy level would be higher. The ε-DP is well-defined because of the measurably of the mapping $\Theta_{\mathfrak{P}}$ as proved in [38].

2.3 State decomposition

State decomposition involves partitioning each node's state into two substates, where only one of these substates is visible to neighboring nodes. **Figure 1** illustrates an example of state decomposition within a given network topology, where i' contains the hidden state information. It is first proposed by Wang [36] to preserve the initial state

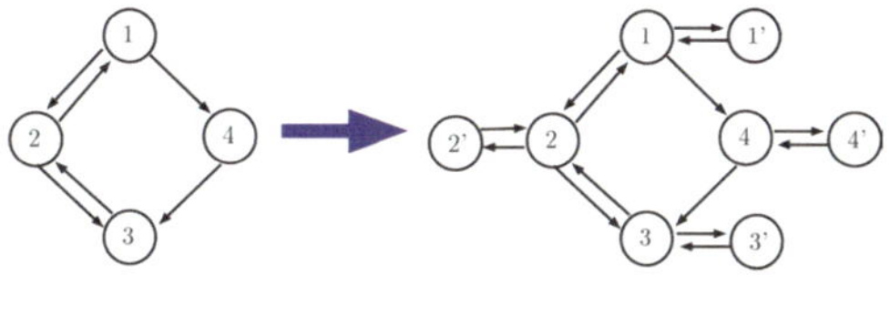

Figure 1.
Demonstration of state decomposition.

privacy in multi-agent systems to reach consensus via an undirected communication network. Chen *et al.* [41] further extended to directed communication networks.

Algorithm 2. SD-Push-Pull [42].

Input: Constant stepsize $\alpha > 0$.
Step 1: Initialization:

1. Node i decides in-graph $\mathcal{G}_R$ and out-graph $\mathcal{G}_{C^\top}$ locally satisfying Assumption 2, and chooses two sub-state weights $\beta_i^1, \beta_i^2 \in (0,1)$, $\forall i \in \mathcal{N}$.

2. Node i picks any $x_i(0), y_i^1(0), y_i^2(0) \in \mathbb{R}^m$, $\theta_i \in \mathbb{R}_+$.

Step 2: At each iteration k, $\forall k \leq K \in \mathbb{N}$, $\forall i \in \mathcal{N}$:

1. Node i pushes $C_{li} y_i^1(k)$ to $l \in \mathcal{N}_{C,i}^{out}$.

2. Node i injects a random noise $\eta_i(k)$ consisting of m zero-mean Laplacian noise independently following $Lap(\theta_i)$ and updates y_i^1, y_i^2 by:

$$\begin{aligned} y_i^1(k+1) &= \sum_j C_{ij} y_j^1(k) + (1-\beta_i^2) y_i^2(k) + \eta_i(k), \\ y_i^2(k+1) &= \beta_i^1 y_i^1(k) + \beta_i^2 y_i^2(k) + \nabla f_i(x_i(k)), \end{aligned} \tag{9}$$

where $Lap(\theta)$ denotes the zero-mean Laplace distribution with probability density function $p_L(x;\theta) = \frac{1}{2\theta} e^{-\frac{|x|}{\theta}}$.

1. Node i pulls $x_j(k) - \alpha\left(y_j^1(k+1) - y_i^1(k)\right)$ from its in-neighbors $j \in \mathcal{N}_{R,i}^{in}$.

2. Node i updates x_i following:

$$x_i(k+1) = \sum_j R_{ij}\left(x_j(k) - \alpha\left(y_j^1(k+1) - y_i^1(k)\right)\right). \tag{10}$$

In SD-Push-Pull outlined in Algorithm 2 [42], the hidden node state $y_i^2(k+1)$ includes the sensitive information of the local gradient function, i.e., $\nabla f_i(x_i(k))$. Since the hidden node state is not shared over the communication network, the private information is protected from being leaked. Although this sensitive information might be revealed through the shared information $y_i^1(k+1)$, noise $\eta_i(k)$ is injected to obscure the data. The effect of this noise on both performance and privacy will be discussed in the following section.

3. Tradeoff between performance and privacy

3.1 Two impossible results of PP-DOAGT

An impossible result between exact convergence, even in the distribution sense, and DP of PP-DOAGT is proved in [38]. This result extends the impossibility findings of [24] and is more challenging than the private consensus problem discussed in [43].

This is because our protection considers the gradient over the entire domain, rather than just a single point.

Theorem 1.1 (First Dilemma) [38] For any given $\{\alpha_k\}_{k\in\mathbb{N}}$, R, C, γ, ϖ and initial state s_0, PP-DOAGT preserves ε-DP for some $\delta, \varepsilon > 0$, and that

$$\lim_{k\to\infty} \mathbf{P}[\|x_i(k) - x^*\|_1 \geq \varepsilon] = 0, \forall i \in \mathcal{N}, \tag{11}$$

cannot hold simultaneously.

For convenience, $\|x_i(k) - x^*\|_1 = o_p(1)$ indicates that $\lim_{k\to\infty}\mathbf{P}[\|x_i(k) - x^*\|_1 \geq \varepsilon] = 0$ for any $\varepsilon > 0$.

It is worth to mention that the statement of Theorem 1 holds universally, regardless of the noise distribution and the choice of noise-to-output mapping $\Theta_{\mathfrak{P}}$, as long as the mapping is continuous and bijective. In other words, this impossibility result applies to a broader range of distributed optimization algorithms other than the one described in (7). Specifically, Assumption 1 and state evolution (7) represent a special case that satisfies that $\Theta_{\mathfrak{P}}$ is continuous and bijective. Consequently, a PP-DOAGT cannot achieve both ε-DP and optimal point convergence in distribution simultaneously.

Given that convergence in distribution is the least strict form of exact convergence, an ε-DP PP-DOAGT cannot achieve exact optimality in any sense, such as the almost surely convergence result as proved in [24]. This leads us to another question: Is it possible to achieve ε-DP while ensuring that PP-DOAGT converges in distribution to a bounded neighborhood of the optimum, i.e., $\|x_i(k) - x^*\|_1 = O_p(1), \forall i \in \mathcal{N}$? Here, notation $O_p(1)$ represents that $\forall \varepsilon > 0$, there exist finite constants $M(\varepsilon) > 0$ and $K(\varepsilon) > 0$ such that $\mathbf{P}[\|x_i(k) - x^*\| > M(\varepsilon)] < \varepsilon$ for all the following iterations $k > K(\varepsilon)$.

For ease of calculating the probability measure in (8), we assume that the noise distribution satisfies Assumption 4.

Assumption 4. The noises $\zeta_i(k), \eta_i(k) \in \mathbb{R}^m$ are identically independent, consisting of the jth element $\zeta_{i,j}(k)$ and $\eta_{i,j}(k)$, $\forall j \in \mathcal{N}$, which satisfies zero-mean Laplace distribution,

$$\zeta_{i,j}(k) \sim Lap(\theta_{\zeta,k}), \eta_{i,j}(k) \sim Lap(\theta_{\eta,k}). \tag{12}$$

Under this noise distribution, [38] proves that PP-DOAGT is not able to have ε-DP if the selected stepsize sequence is not summable.

Theorem 1.2 (Second Dilemma) [38] PP-DOAGT with any given $\{\alpha_k\}_{k\in\mathbb{N}}$ satisfying $\sum_{k=0}^{\infty}\alpha_k = \infty$ and $\sup_{k\in\mathbb{N}}\alpha_k < \infty$ cannot achieve ε-DP.

The second dilemma sets the stage for a comprehensive examination of privacy and performance under summable stepsize sequences. Other literature does not pay much attention to this condition since it cannot ensure the convergence of DOAGT to their optima because of the incomplete exploration of the state space. Denote $\overline{x}(k) = u^{\mathrm{T}}x(k)$ to be the weighted average at kth iteration, where u is the unique left eigenvalue of R.

Theorem 1.3 (Performance Analysis) [38] Consider PP-DOAGT under Assumptions 1–4. When the variances of noise sequences satisfy $\sum_{k=0}^{\infty}\theta_{\zeta,k}^2 < \infty$, $\sum_{k=0}^{\infty}\frac{\theta_{\eta,k}^2}{\alpha_k} < \infty$, $\sum_{k=0}^{\infty}\alpha_k < \infty$, and the stepsize sequences $\frac{\alpha_k}{\alpha_{k_0}} \geq \beta\lambda^{k-k_0}$ for all positive integers $k > k_0$ with a possible $\lambda \in (q_C, 1)$ and $k_0 \in \mathbb{N}$, the weighted average of local estimates $\overline{x}$ will converge to the neigbouhood of the optimum in distribution, i.e., $\sup_{k\in\mathbb{N}}\mathbf{E}\left[\|\overline{x}(k) - x^{*\mathrm{T}}\|_2^2\right] \leq D_1$ with D_1 bounded. In addition, all the agents local estimate will converge to the weighted average almost surely and from the mean-square perspective.

It is easy to prove that the PP-DOAGT achieves stochastically bounded error under the conditions.

Corollary 1 [38]. When the conditions in Theorem 1.3 hold, we have that each node will converge to a bounded neighborhood of the optimum in distribution under PP-DOAGT.

Sufficient conditions to ensure that PP-DOAGT has ε-DP for any two δ-adjacent distributed optimization problems is summarized in Theorem 1.4.

Theorem 1.4 (Privacy Analysis) [38] Consider PP-DOAGT under the above assumptions. When the following conditions $\sum_{k=0}^{\infty}\alpha_k < \infty$, $D_\eta := \sum_{k=0}^{\infty}\frac{\alpha_k}{\theta_{\eta,k+1}} < \infty$ and $D_\zeta := \sum_{k=0}^{\infty}\frac{\alpha_k}{\theta_{\zeta,k+1}} < \infty$ hold, Algorithm 1 obtains ε-DP for any two δ-adjacent distributed optimization problems, where

$$\varepsilon = \frac{\delta + 2LD}{\gamma\varpi}\left(\varpi D_\eta + 2D_\zeta\right), \tag{13}$$

where

$$D = K \geq \underline{k} \inf \max\left\{\frac{\max\limits_{0\leq i<K}\alpha_i(\delta + L\xi_i) + \overline{\alpha}_K\delta}{\varpi\gamma - 2\overline{\alpha}_K L}, \max_{0\leq i<K}\frac{\xi_i}{2}\right\}. \tag{14}$$

with

$$\underline{k} := \min\left\{k \middle| \alpha_t < \frac{\varpi\gamma}{2L}, \forall t \geq k\right\}, \overline{\alpha}_k := \sup_{t\geq k}\alpha_t. \tag{15}$$

By Theorem 1.3 and 1.4, we conclude that it is possible to design $\{\alpha_k\}_{k\in\mathbb{N}}$, $\theta_{\zeta,k}$ and $\theta_{\eta,k}$ such that PP-DOAGT can ensure $\|x_i(k) - x^*\|_1 = O_p(1)$ while achieving ε-DP, provided that $\sum_{k=0}^{\infty}\alpha_k < \infty$. This is formally presented in Corollary 2.

Corollary 2 [38]. Consider PP-DOAGT under the above Assumptions. When the following conditions $\sum_{k=0}^{\infty}\alpha_k < \infty$, $\sum_{k=0}^{\infty}\theta_{\zeta,k}^2 < \infty$, $\sum_{k=0}^{\infty}\frac{\theta_{\eta,k}^2}{\alpha_k} < \infty$, $\sum_{k=0}^{\infty}\frac{\alpha_k}{\theta_{\eta,k+1}} < \infty$, $\sum_{k=0}^{\infty}\frac{\alpha_k}{\theta_{\zeta,k+1}} < \infty$, and $\frac{\alpha_k}{\alpha_{k_0}} \geq \beta\lambda^{k-k_0}$ for all natural number $k > k_0$ with a possible $\lambda \in (q_C, 1)$ and a natural number k_0 hold, PP-DOAGT achieves stochastically bounded error while satisfies ε-DP with ε given by (13) and (14) simultaneously.

To sum up, the tradeoff between privacy and convergence under PP-DOAGT is illustrated in **Figure 2**. The dark blue areas represent where PP-DOAGT achieves ε-

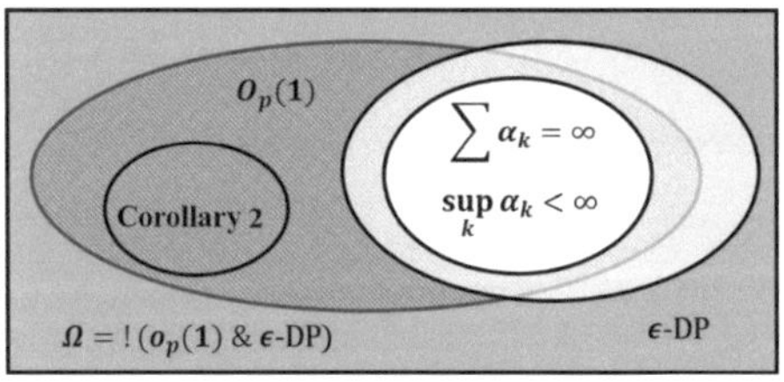

Figure 2.
The tradeoff between performance and privacy under PP-DOAGT.

DP, while the areas with blue lines indicate where PP-DOAGT achieves stochastically bounded error.

3.2 Performance and privacy analysis of SD-push-pull

Different from the first part, which considers protecting function gradients over infinite iterations, SD-Push-Pull only considers protecting the sensitive information over finite iterations till K steps [42]. However, due to the allowable constant stepsize, a linear convergence to a neighborhood of optimum distribution at an exponential rate can be achieved under SD-Push-Pull. Theorem 1.5 demonstrates the convergence characteristics.

Theorem 1.5 [Performance Analysis] [42] Consider SD-Push-Pull under the above assumptions. When the constant stepsize α follows the below condition:

$$\alpha \leq \min\left\{\sqrt{\frac{1-\sigma_R^2}{6c_5}}, \sqrt{\frac{1-\sigma_C^2}{6c_{10}}}, \sqrt{\frac{2d_3}{d_2+\sqrt{d_2^2+4d_1d_3}}}\right\}, \tag{16}$$

Then, the supremum of the expectation of the difference between each node's estimate and the optimum or the average converges to $\lim\sup_{k\to\infty}\mathbf{E}\left[\|\overline{x}(k)-x^{*\top}\|_2^2\right]$ or $\lim\sup_{k\to\infty}\mathbf{E}\left[\|\|x(k)-\mathbf{1}\overline{x}(k)\|_2^2\right]$, respectively, with the linear convergence rate $O\left(\rho(A)^k\right)$, where $\rho(A)<1$. Furthermore, specific mathematical forms of the above notions are given in [42].

In the above theorem, the specific forms of scalars $d_1, d_2, d_3, c_5, c_{10}$ are also seen in detail in [42].

Next, the privacy level of SD-Push-Pull is quantified using DP. Since SD-Push-Pull considers only finite iteration steps and all the gradients of local objective functions $\|\nabla f_i(x_i(k))\|_2$ are bounded. For convenience, let us assume the bound is U, i.e., $\|\nabla f_i(x_i(k))\|_2 \leq U, \forall i \in \mathcal{N}$ and $\forall k=0,1,\ldots,K$. The ε-DP is guaranteed by adding noise satisfying Theorem 1.6.

Theorem 1.6 [Privacy Analysis] [42] Consider SD-Push-Pull under Assumptions 1–3. Under a finite iteration number $k \leq K$, SD-Push-Pull preserve ε_i-DP for each node i's local objective function when the noise variance satisfies

$$\theta_i \geq \frac{2\sqrt{m}UK}{\varepsilon_i}. \tag{17}$$

In other words, if all nodes choose $\theta_i=\theta$, SD-Push-Pull can preserve ε-DP with $\varepsilon=\frac{2\sqrt{m}UK}{\theta}$. Note that the privacy level can be improved by increasing the noise variance θ; however, the performance accuracy would become arbitrarily low. The tradeoff between privacy and performance of SD-Push-Pull is shown in Theorems 1.5 and 1.6.

3.3 Scalability issues

We note that the privacy-preservation steps are Step 2.1 in Algorithm 1 and Step 2.2 in Algorithm 2 by simple adding operation. In addition, the algorithm will converge to a neighborhood of the optimum within finite step K by Theorem 1.3 and Theorem 1.5. Therefore, the whole added privacy-preservation steps increase linearly with the number of nodes, unlike cryptographic methods, which require the computational burden increase exponentially with respect to the node number. The two proposed methods are more desirable to be implemented in a large-scale of network in different areas, which will be included in the next section.

4. Application scenarios

A wealth of information about the underlying model is carried by the gradient of a cost function. This privacy concern has attracted increasing interest in areas such as deep learning [44, 45], collaborative computing [46], energy management [47], and traffic transportation [48].

Take classification problems in machine learning as an example. Suppose a multi-agent system seeks to determine an optimal weight for features h_i by the training labels z_i to minimize the sum of classification error, given by $x^* = \arg\min_{x\in\mathbb{R}^m}\sum_{i=1}^{N}\frac{1}{2}\left(h_i^\top x - z_i\right)^2$, while each agent holds (h_i, z_i) as sensitive data. It is worth noting that gradient information $\nabla f_i(x) = h_i^\top x - z_i$ may reveal the agents' personal preferences about some features. Concerns about privacy leakage of sensitive information may discourage agents from sharing their data to enhance learning performance.

The effectiveness of the provided two algorithms is demonstrated via a numerical ridge regression problem, i.e.,

$$\min_{x\in\mathbb{R}^m}\sum_{i=1}^{N} f_i(x) = \sum_{i=1}^{N}\left(\left(h_i^\top x - z_i\right)^2 + \rho\|x\|_2^2\right). \tag{18}$$

Here, ρ indicates a regulation penalty parameter. Consider $\rho = 0.01$ and there exists $_{\text{five}}$ agents collaboratively solving the above optimization problem distributively. The communication network depicted in **Figure 3** highlights Agent 3 in a central role. Agent 3 exclusively transmitted information to agents 2 and 4 and then compiles gradient estimates from its in-neighbors 2 and 5. The other agents form a cyclic communication topology, with connections established as $1 \to 4 \to 5 \to 2 \to 1$. Let the mixing weights R, C be: $\forall i$, $R_{ii} = 0.5$ and $R_{ij} = \frac{1}{2|\mathcal{N}_{R,i}^{\text{in}}|}$, $\forall j \in \mathcal{N}_{R,i}^{\text{in}}$; $C_{ii} = 0.5$, $C_{ji} = \frac{1}{2|\mathcal{N}_{C,i}^{\text{out}}|}$, $\forall j \in \mathcal{N}_{C,i}^{\text{out}}$. It is worth to mention that neither G_R nor $\left(\mathrm{G}_{C^\top}\right)$ satisfies strongly connected condition.

To begin with, we let agent $i\in\mathcal{N}$ draw the variables $h_i \in [-1, 1]^m$ and $\tilde{x}_i \in [0, 10]^m$ randomly following uniform distributions. The observed outputs z_i can be then calculated as $z_i = h_i^\top \tilde{x}_i + v_i$, where v_i follows Gaussian distribution with zero-mean and variance 25. The problem's optimal solution is unique, to be specific, $x^* = \left(\sum_{i=1}^{N} h_i h_i^\top + N\rho I\right)^{-1}\sum_{i=1}^{N} h_i h_i^\top \tilde{x}_i$.

4.1 Demonstration of PP-DOAGT

Let $\varpi = \gamma = 0.9$ and $\alpha_0 = 0.1 < \frac{\varpi\gamma}{2L}$. From Corollary 2, consider the special choice of exponential convergence $\alpha_k = 0.1q^k$, $\theta_{\zeta,k} = \theta_{\eta,k} = q_\eta^k$. Then one has $\varepsilon = \frac{3.6915}{q_\eta - q}\delta$. With

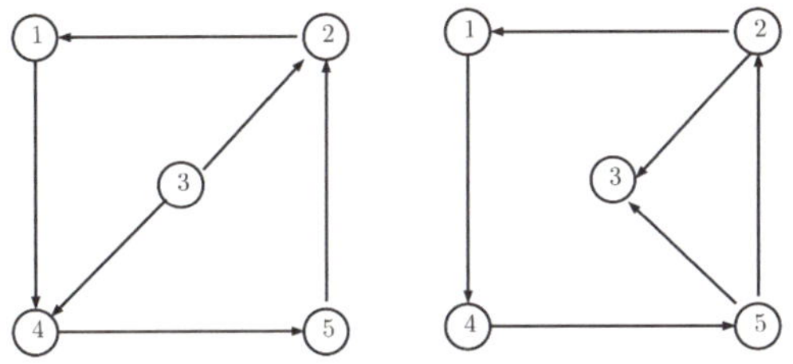

Figure 3.
Communication topology demonstration, where the left (right) is the communication digraph $\mathcal{G}_R(\mathcal{G}_{C^\top})$.

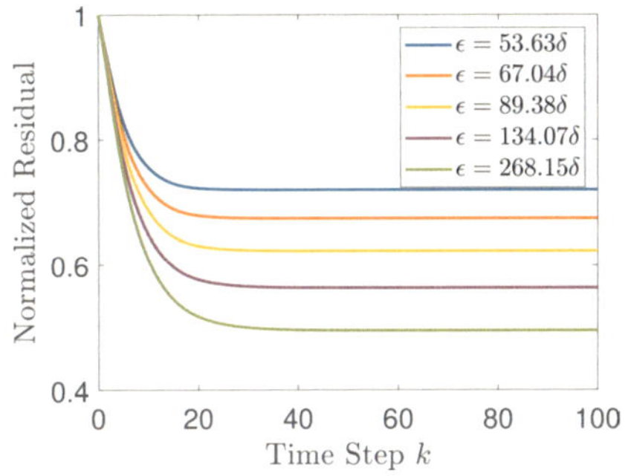

Figure 4.
The performance accuracy versus time steps under the different privacy level.

$q_\eta = 0.93$ fixed, the conditions for achieving ε-DP and $O_p(1)$ are satisfied if $0.8682 < q < 0.93$.

We evaluate performance by comparing the normalized residual $\frac{1}{N}\mathbf{E}\left[\sum_{i=1}^{N}\frac{\|x_i(k)-x^*\|_1}{\|x_i(0)-x^*\|_1}\right]$ under PP-DOAGT with different convergence stepsize ratio averaging over 100 simulation results under cases: $q = \{0.87, 0.88, 0.89, 0.90, 0.91\}$, to demonstrate the tradeoff.

When q increases, the term $(1-q)(q-q_c)$ increases in this domain, which indicates that when the stepsize converges slower, a smaller performance accuracy bound D_1 can be obtained. However, this increased performance sacrifices privacy since ε also grows when q increases, weakening the privacy level. The above results inherently demonstrates a tradeoff between privacy and performance, as depicted in **Figure 4**.

4.2 Demonstration of SD-push-pull

Let the weights between two substates, β_i^1, β_i^2 be 0.01 and 0.5 for each agent $i \in \mathcal{N}$, respectively. Assume that each agent has the same privacy level ε and let $\delta = 10$. The tradeoff between privacy and performance over finite time step $K = 5000$ are demonstrated in **Figure 5** for three cases: $\varepsilon = \{1, 5, 10\}$, averaging over 50 simulation results. This figure depicts that Algorithm 2 converges to a neighborhood of the optimum in expectation to guarantee ε-DP. Additionally, higher privacy level also corrupt the performance accuracy.

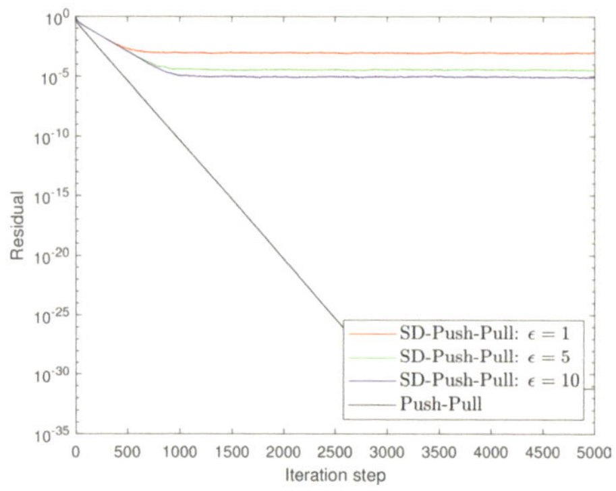

Figure 5.
The performance accuracy versus time steps under the different privacy level.

5. Conclusions

In this chapter, we explore techniques for preserving privacy in distributed optimization problems via directed communication networks. Two algorithms, namely, PP-DOAGT and SD-Push-Pull, are introduced to navigate the tradeoff between performance and privacy. Although PP-DOAGT ensures privacy over an infinite number of iterations, it reveals two significant limitations that highlight the inherent tradeoff between performance and privacy. Due to the second dilemma, analyses of tradeoff between ε-DP and performance are conducted under summable stepsize sequences. In contrast, SD-Push-Pull focuses on privacy guarantees over finite iterations. Utilizing state-decomposition, this method targets convergence to a neighborhood of the optimum at a linear convergence rate with a constant stepsize under certain conditions. Various application scenarios demonstrate the effectiveness of these two algorithms in preserving privacy while maintaining performance.

Acknowledgements

The chapter is supported by the National Research Foundation of Singapore under its Medium-Sized Center for Advanced Robotics Technology Innovation and by Naval Group Far East Pte Ltd. via an RCA with NTU.

Abbreviations

DOAGT	Distributed optimization algorithm with gradient tracking
DP	Differential privacy
PP-DOAGT	Privacy-preserving DOAGT
SD-Push-Pull	State-decomposition-based push-pull

Author details

Lingying Huang[1,2]*, Rong Su[1], Xiaomeng Chen[2] and Junfeng Wu[3]

1 School of Electrical and Electronic Engineering, Nanyang Technological University, Singapore

2 Department of Electronic and Computer Engineering, Hong Kong University of Science and Technology, Clear Water Bay, Kowloon, Hong Kong

3 School of Data Science, Chinese University of Hong Kong (Shenzhen), Shenzhen, China

*Address all correspondence to: lingying.huang@ntu.edu.sg

References

[1] Braun P, Grüne L, Kellett CM, Weller SR, Worthmann K. A distributed optimization algorithm for the predictive control of smart grids. IEEE Transactions on Automatic Control. 2016;**61**(12): 3898-3911

[2] Predd JB, Kulkarni SB, Poor HV. Distributed learning in wireless sensor networks. IEEE Signal Processing Magazine. 2006;**23**(4):56-69

[3] Schizas ID, Ribeiro A, Giannakis GB. Consensus in ad hoc WSNs with noisy links-part I: Distributed estimation of deterministic signals. IEEE Transactions on Signal Processing. 2007;**56**(1): 350-364

[4] Ling Q, Tian Z. Decentralized sparse signal recovery for compressive sleeping wireless sensor networks. IEEE Transactions on Signal Processing. 2010; **58**(7):3816-3827

[5] Dougherty S, Guay M. An extremum-seeking controller for distributed optimization over sensor networks. IEEE Transactions on Automatic Control. 2016;**62**(2):928-933

[6] Mohebifard R, Hajbabaie A. Distributed optimization and coordination algorithms for dynamic traffic metering in urban street networks. IEEE Transactions on Intelligent Transportation Systems. 2018;**20**(5):1930-1941

[7] Estrin D, Govindan R, Heidemann J, Kumar S. Next century challenges: Scalable coordination in sensor networks. In: Proceedings of the Fifth Annual ACM/IEEE International Conference on Mobile Computing and Networking. New York, NY, United States: Association for Computing Machinery; 1999. pp. 263-270

[8] Nedic A, Ozdaglar A. Distributed subgradient methods for multi-agent optimization. IEEE Transactions on Automatic Control. 2009;**54**(1):48-61

[9] Ram SS, Nedić A, Veeravalli VV. Distributed stochastic subgradient projection algorithms for convex optimization. Journal of Optimization Theory and Applications. 2010;**147**(3): 516-545

[10] Duchi JC, Agarwal A, Wainwright MJ. Dual averaging for distributed optimization: Convergence analysis and network scaling. IEEE Transactions on Automatic Control. 2011;**57**(3):592-606

[11] Shi W, Ling Q, Wu G, Yin W. Extra: An exact first-order algorithm for decentralized consensus optimization. SIAM Journal on Optimization. 2015; **25**(2):944-966

[12] Tsianos KI, Lawlor S, Rabbat MG. Push-sum distributed dual averaging for convex optimization. In: 2012 IEEE 51st IEEE Conference on Decision and Control (CDC). Grand Wailea; IEEE; 2012. pp. 5453-5458

[13] Xi C, Khan UA. Dextra: A fast algorithm for optimization over directed graphs. IEEE Transactions on Automatic Control. 2017;**62**(10):4980-4993

[14] Xi C, Mai VS, Xin R, Abed EH, Khan UA. Linear convergence in optimization over directed graphs with row-stochastic matrices. IEEE Transactions on Automatic Control. 2018;**63**(10):3558-3565

[15] Xin R, Khan UA. A linear algorithm for optimization over directed graphs with geometric convergence. IEEE

Control Systems Letters. 2018;**2**(3): 315-320

[16] Pu S, Shi W, Xu J, Nedic A. Push-pull gradient methods for distributed optimization in networks. IEEE Transactions on Automatic Control. 2020,**66**(1):1-16

[17] Pu S. A robust gradient tracking method for distributed optimization over directed networks. arXiv preprint arXiv:2003.13980. 2020

[18] Aysal TC, Barner KE. Sensor data cryptography in wireless sensor networks. IEEE Transactions on Information Forensics and Security. 2008;**3**(2):273-289

[19] Dwork C, McSherry F, Nissim K, Smith A. Calibrating noise to sensitivity in private data analysis. In: Theory of Cryptography Conference. New York, NY, United States: Springer; 2006. pp. 265-284

[20] Dwork C. Differential privacy: A survey of results. In: International Conference on Theory and Applications of Models of Computation. Xian, China: Springer; 2008. pp. 1-19

[21] Huang Z, Mitra S, Dullerud G. Differentially private iterative synchronous consensus. In: Proceedings of the 2012 ACM Workshop on Privacy in the Electronic Society. New York, NY, United States: Association for Computing Machinery; 2012. pp. 81-90

[22] Huang Z, Mitra S, Vaidya N. Differentially private distributed optimization. In: Proceedings of the 2015 International Conference on Distributed Computing and Networking. New York, NY, United States: Association for Computing Machinery; 2015. pp. 1-10

[23] Ding T, Zhu S, He J, Chen C, Guan X. Consensus-based distributed optimization in multi-agent systems: Convergence and differential privacy. In: 2018 IEEE Conference on Decision and Control (CDC). Miami Beach, FL, USA: IEEE; 2018. pp. 3409-3414

[24] Ding T, Zhu S, He J, Chen C, Guan X-P. Differentially private distributed optimization via state and direction perturbation in multi-agent systems. IEEE Transactions on Automatic Control. 2021;**67**(2):722-737

[25] Ghabcheloo R, Pascoal A, Silvestre C, Kaminer I. Coordinated path following control of multiple wheeled robots with directed communication links. In: Proceedings of the 44th IEEE Conference on Decision and Control. Seville, Spain: IEEE; 2005. pp. 7084-7089

[26] Yang S, Tan S, Xu J-X. Consensus based approach for economic dispatch problem in a smart grid. IEEE Transactions on Power Systems. 2013; **28**(4):4416-4426

[27] Mao S, Tang Y, Dong Z, Meng K, Dong ZY, Qian F. A privacy preserving distributed optimization algorithm for economic dispatch over time-varying directed networks. IEEE Transactions on Industrial Informatics. 2020;**17**(3): 1689-1701

[28] Zhu J, Xu C, Guan J, Wu DO. Differentially private distributed online algorithms over time-varying directed networks. IEEE Transactions on Signal and Information Processing over Networks. 2018;**4**(1):4-17

[29] Xiong Y, Xu J, You K, Liu J, Wu L. Privacy preserving distributed online optimization over unbalanced digraphs via subgradient rescaling. IEEE Transactions on Control of Network Systems. 2020;**7**(3):1366-1378

[30] Gao H, Wang Y, Nedić A. Dynamics based privacy preservation in decentralized optimization. Automatica. 2023;**151**:110878

[31] Wang Y, Başar T. Gradient-tracking based distributed optimization with guaranteed optimality under noisy information sharing. IEEE Transactions on Automatic Control. 2022;**68**(8):4796-4811

[32] Fung BC, Wang K, Fu AW-C, Philip SY. Introduction to Privacy-Preserving Data Publishing: Concepts and Techniques. Boca Raton, Florida: CRC Press; 2010

[33] Gedik B, Liu L. Protecting location privacy with personalized k-anonymity: Architecture and algorithms. IEEE Transactions on Mobile Computing. 2007;**7**(1):1-18

[34] Lu Y, Zhu M. Privacy preserving distributed optimization using homomorphic encryption. Automatica. 2018;**96**:314-325

[35] Ding W, Zhou J, Yang W, Tang Y. An efficient encoding mechanism against eavesdropper with side channel information. Automatica. 2023;**153**:111062

[36] Wang Y. Privacy-preserving average consensus via state decomposition. IEEE Transactions on Automatic Control. 2019;**64**(11):4711-4716

[37] Godsil C, Royle GF. Algebraic Graph Theory. Vol. 207. Berlin/Heidelberg, Germany: Springer Science & Business Media; 2001

[38] Huang L, Wu J, Shi D, Dey S, Shi L. Differential privacy in distributed optimization with gradient tracking. IEEE Transactions on Automatic Control. 2024;**69**(9):5727-5742

[39] Du W, Yao L, Wu D, Li X, Liu G, Yang T. Accelerated distributed energy management for microgrids. In: 2018 IEEE Power & Energy Society General Meeting (PESGM). Vol. 2018. Portland, Oregon, USA: IEEE; 2018. pp. 1-5

[40] Nedic A, Olshevsky A, Shi W. Achieving geometric convergence for distributed optimization over time-varying graphs. SIAM Journal on Optimization. 2017;**27**(4):2597-2633

[41] Chen X, Huang L, Ding K, Dey S, Shi L. Privacy-preserving push-sum average consensus via state decomposition. IEEE Transactions on Automatic Control. 2023;**68**(12):7974-7981

[42] Chen X, Huang L, He L, Dey S, Shi L. A differentially private method for distributed optimization in directed networks via state decomposition. IEEE Transactions on Control of Network Systems. 2023;**10**(4):2165-2177

[43] Nozari E, Tallapragada P, Cortés J. Differentially private distributed convex optimization via functional perturbation. IEEE Transactions on Control of Network Systems. 2016;**5**(1):395-408

[44] Abadi M, Chu A, Goodfellow I, McMahan HB, Mironov I, Talwar K, et al. Deep learning with differential privacy. In: Proceedings of the 2016 ACM SIGSAC Conference on Computer and Communications Security. New York, NY, United States: Association for Computing Machinery; 2016. pp. 308-318

[45] Melis L, Song C, De Cristofaro E, Shmatikov V. Exploiting unintended feature leakage in collaborative learning. In: 2019 IEEE Symposium on Security and Privacy (SP). Vol. 2019. San Francisco, CA: IEEE; pp. 691-706

[46] Konečný J, McMahan HB, Yu FX, Richtárik P, Suresh AT, Bacon D. Federated learning: Strategies for improving communication efficiency. 2016. arXiv preprint arXiv:1610.05492

[47] Liu E, Cheng P. Achieving privacy protection using distributed load scheduling: A randomized approach. IEEE Transactions on Smart Grid. 2017; **8**(5):2460-2473

[48] Li H, Dán G, Nahrstedt K. Portunes+: Privacy-preserving fast authentication for dynamic electric vehicle charging. IEEE Transactions on Smart Grid. 2016;**8**(5):2305-2313

Chapter 4

Information Privacy Rights in India: A Study of the Digital Personal Data Protection Act, 2023

Ajay Kumar Bisht and Neeruganti Shanmuka Sreenivasulu

Abstract

The widespread threats to the information privacy of the individuals in the digitally connected world have motivated the authors to examine the efficacy of the provisions of the newly enacted law of India, namely the Digital Personal Data Protection Act, 2023 (in short being called the DPDP Act, 2023). The objective of the chapter is to evaluate the adequacy and the appropriateness of the provisions that guarantee the information privacy rights of the individuals. After the introductory section, the relevant definitions listed under Section 2 of the Act are examined in the second section of this chapter. Thereafter, the obligations cast upon the data fiduciaries under chapter II of the Act will be discussed in the Section 3 of this chapter. In the fourth section, the rights of the individuals laid down in the chapter III of the Act will be examined. The penal provision for violation of the rights of the individuals will be discussed in the fifth section. In the sixth section, the enforcement mechanism will be examined. The last section, number seventh, will be devoted to the suggestions made by the authors and the conclusions arrived at. The authors suggest that a specific provision may be added in the Digital Data Protection Act, 2023 with the heading "Right to data portability." A dedicated provision on the portability would sensitize the data ecosystem to take the responsibility of maintaining the data in a structured, commonly used, and machine-readable format. The authors further suggest the incorporation of a specific provision on "the right to be forgotten" in the DPD Act, 2023 on the lines of the provision proposed by the Committee of Experts in clause 27 of the PDP Bill, 2018 and the provision proposed by the Joint Committee of Parliament in clause 20 of the D.P. Bill, 2021. Further, the authors suggest the incorporation of a provision on compensation to the person who suffered harm due to the violation of the law of data protection. The authors further suggest the addition of a provision that a separate Tribunal dedicated to decide the cases under the Act may be constituted. The authors conclude that the rights of information privacy are largely covered in the DPDP Act, 2023 of India and the five changes suggested in the Section 6.1 (infra) are the only five improvements required to effectively protect the information privacy rights under the Digital Personal Data Protection Act, 2023.

Keywords: privacy rights, consent, lawful processing, privacy violation, penalties

1. Introduction

The widespread threats to the information privacy of the individuals in the digitally connected world have motivated the authors to examine the efficacy of the provisions of the newly enacted law of India, namely the Digital Personal Data Protection Act, 2023 (in short being called the DPDP Act, 2023). The objective of the chapter is to evaluate the adequacy and the appropriateness of the provisions that guarantee the information privacy rights of the individuals and the enforcement of those rights.

After this introductory section, the relevant definitions listed under Section 2 of the Act are examined in the second section of this chapter. Thereafter, the obligations cast upon the data fiduciaries under chapter II of the Act will be discussed in the Section 3 of this chapter. In the fourth section, the rights of the individuals laid down in the chapter III of the Act will be examined. The penal provision for violation of the rights of the individuals will be discussed in the fifth section. The enforcement mechanism stipulated in the Act is discussed critically in the sixth section. The last section, that is, number seventh, will be devoted to the suggestions made by the authors and the conclusions arrived at. In all these sections, the provisions of the DPDP Act, 2023 will be critically examined with reference to the relevant documents including the following:

i. The Modernized Convention 108 of the Council of Europe of the year 2018 (also called Convention 108+),

ii. The General Data Protection Regulation of the European Union of the year 2016 (also called GDPR),

iii. The judgment dated 24th August, 2017 of the nine judge bench of the Supreme Court of India in WP (Civil) No 494 of 2012 titled Justice K.S. Puttaswamy v. Union of India (in short being called Puttaswamy, 2017),

iv. The report of the year 2018 of the Committee of Experts headed by Justice B.N. Srikrishna, constituted by the Government of India in the year 2017, to draft a data protection law for India (in short being called report of the Committee of Experts),

v. The Personal Data Protection Bill, 2018 recommended to the Government of India, by the Committee of Experts headed by Justice B.N. Srikrishna (in short being called PDP Bill, 2018),

vi. The Data Protection Bill, 2021 recommended by the Joint Parliamentary Committee of Parliament of India (in short being called DP Bill, 2021).

- Absence of case law under the Act: since the rules under the DPDP Act, 2023 have not been notified till the writing of this script, the Act has not been implemented till date and so case-law under the DPDP Act, 2023 is not available.

2. Important definitions

In the digital medium, information primary means protection of personal data. Therefore, we will begin with the analysis of the definitions data, personal data, data principal, data fiduciary, data processor, and processing.

2.1 "Data"

Section 2(h) of the DPDP Act, 2023 defines "data" as something that the human beings or the automated systems can communicate, interpret or process ([1], p. 02). The "something" here implies any information, concept, fact, opinion, or instruction ([1], p. 02). Neither the Convention 108+ of the Council of Europe, nor the GDPR of the European Union define the term data.

The term "data" is defined in clause 3(12) of the PDP Bill, 2018 in the same terms as in the section 2(h) of the DPDP Act, 2023 ([2], p. 03). The Joint Committee of Parliament had suggested the definition of "data" which is in line with the definition in section 2(h) of the DPD Act, 2023 ([3], p. 03). In common parlance in India, the Joint Committee of Parliament is also called **JPC** in short.

The definition of the term "data" in the section 2(o) the Information Technology Act, 2000 is also within the broad contours of the definition stipulated in sec 2(h) of the DPD Act, 2023 ([4], p. 07).

Thus, the authors find that the DPD Act, 2023 has proposed a comprehensive and clear definition of the term "data" in section 2(h).

2.2 "Personal data"

The section 2(t) of the DPD Act, 2023 defines any data about an individual which identifies that person as "personal data" ([1], p. 02). The article 2.a of the Convention 108+ of the Council of Europe defines "personal data" as any information about an identified or an identifiable individual ([5], p. 07). The GDPR of the European Union defines "personal data" in the article 4(1) in similar language as Convention 108+ as any information about an identifiable or identified individual ([6], p. L119/33).

The Committee of Experts had evolved a detailed definition of "personal data" defining it in clause 3(29) of the PDP Bill, 2018 as data about or relating to a natural person who is directly or indirectly identifiable ([2], p. 05).

The Joint Committee of the Parliament had recommended in clause 3(33), a definition of "personal data" which added to the definition proposed in the PDP Bill, 2018, by including 'any inference drawn from such data for the purpose of profiling' ([3], p. 06).

The authors find that the definition of "personal data" in the DPDP Act, 2023 is short as compared to the definitions proposed in earlier legislative proposal of India. However, the definition being in general terms is on the lines of the shorter definitions of the European regional documents namely the Convention 108+ and the GDPR; it is expected to be expansive in its scope and so, would serve the purpose.

2.3 "Data principal"

The person whose personal data is in issue is defined in section 2(j) as "data principal" ([1], p. 02). The section 2(j) further qualifies the definition by making provision that lawful guardian will be the data principal where the personal data relates to children or persons with disability ([1], p. 02). The Convention 108+ calls such person "data subject." The article 2.a of the Convention 108+ defines "data subject" as the identified or identifiable individual whose personal data is in issue ([5], p. 07). The article 4(1) of the GDPR defines "data subject" in the same language as the article 2.a of the Convention 108+ ([6], p. L119/33).

The Committee of Experts headed by Justice B.N. Srikrishna was of the view that the autonomy of the individuals in relation to their personal data needs to be enhanced and that there is an urgent need to remove the existing imbalance in the bargaining power of the individuals vis-à-vis the entities that process and control data ([7], p. 07-08). The Committee of Experts, therefore, suggested the name "data principal" for the individual whose personal data is in issue ([7], p. 08). Accordingly, clause 3(14) of the PDP Bill, 2018 defined "data principal" as the natural person to whom the personal data in issue relates ([2], p. 03). The Committee of Experts, therefore, made the **individual** the focal point of the regime of data protection and so, the Committee proposed the word "**data principal**" for the individual who is referred to as "**data subject**" in the regional documents of Europe, namely Convention 108+ and the G.D.P. R.

The JPC agreed with the definition proposed by the Committee of Experts and so the definition in clause 3(16) of the DP Bill, 2021 defined "data principal" as the natural person whose personal date is in issue ([3], p. 04). The authors, thus, found that the emphasis on the individual is rightly reinforced by calling him/her as "data principal" instead of "data subject." The information privacy rights of the individual will be protected better under the definition of "data principal" provided in 2(j) of the DPDP Act, 2023.

2.4 "Data fiduciary"

The section 2(i) of the DPDP Act, 2023 defines data fiduciary as the person who alone or jointly with others, decides the purpose and the mechanism of processing of personal data ([1], p. 02).

The European regional documents use the term data controller and so, the article 2.d of the Convention 108+ defines "controller" as the natural or legal person, public authority, service agency, or any other organization which alone or in conjunction with others, decides the purpose and the means of processing ([5], p. 07). The article 4(7) of the GDPR defines "controller" more elaborately than the definition in article 2.d of Convention 108+ by adding the classification that the purpose and means of processing would be decided in accordance with the law of the Member State or the law of the European Union ([6], p. L119/33).

The Committee of Experts of India was of the opinion that in a free and fair digital economy, the relationship between the individual and the entity processing the data should be based on mutual trust ([7], p. 08). The Committee, therefore, recommended in clause 3(13) of the PDP Bill, 2018 the definition of "data fiduciary" as a person, including the State, or company, any juristic entity or any individual who alone or jointly with other decide the purpose and mechanism of processing ([2], p. 03).

The JPC in clause 3(16) of DP Bill, 2021 suggested that definition of "data fiduciary" as was suggested by the Committee of Experts in the clause 3(14) of the PDP Bill, 2018 ([3], p. 04).

The authors find that the language for the "data fiduciary" in the DP Act, 2023 is on same lines as suggested by the Committee of Experts and the Joint Committee of Parliament. Further, the authors find that the concept of **fiduciary relationship,** a better approach toward instilling an element of trust, and thereby, reduces the existing inequality between the data principal and the data controller.

2.5 "Data processor"

The section 2(k) of the DPDP Act, 2023 defines "data processor" as the person who processes personal data on behalf of the data fiduciary ([1], p. 02).

The article Convention 2.e of the Convention 108+ defines "processor" as a natural or juristic person, public authority, service agency, or any other organization which process personal data on behalf of the data controller ([5], p. 07). The article 4(7) of the GDPR defines "data processor" in the same language as the article 2.e of the Convention 108+ ([6], p. L119/33).

The Committee of Exerts proposed the definition of the processor in clause 3(15) of the PDP Bill, 2018 on the lines of the definitions in article 2.e of the Convention 108+, but with the exception of an employee of the "data fiduciary" ([2], p. 03). The JPC in the clause 3(17) removed the exception of employee from the definition proposed in the PDP Bill, 2018 and added the non-governmental organization in the category of the data processors ([3], p. 04).

The authors find that the definition of "data processor" in section 2(k) of the DPDP Act, 2023 appropriately includes the required categories.

2.6 "Processing"

The section 2(x) of the DPDP Act, 2023 defines "processing" of personal data in a very detailed manner. It says processing means wholly or partly automated operations performed on digital personal data including the collection, storage, adoption, sharing, erasure, or destruction ([1], p. 03).

The article 2.b of the Convention 108+ defines "data processing" as operations performed on personal data including collection, storage, alteration, disclosure, and logical operations or arithmetical operations on personal data ([5], p. 07).

The article 4(2) of the GDPR bases the definition of processing on the article 2.b of the Convention 108+ but adds the clarification with the words "whether or not by automated means" ([6], p. L119/33). The definition in the GDPR thus includes manual processing in the category of processing.

The Committee of Experts recommended in clause 3(32) of the PDP Bill, 2018 the definition of processing on the lines of the definition of processing laid down in article 2.b of the Convention 108+ ([2], p. 05).

The JPC recommended in clause (36) of the DP Bill, 2021 a definition of processing on the lines of the definition in 3(32) of the PDP, 2018 ([3], p. 07).

The authors, thus, find that the definition of processing in the DPDP Act, 2023 is an improvement over the definitions proposed by the Committee of Experts and the Joint Committee of Parliament. By defining "processing" on the lines of the definition in article 4(2) of the GDPR, the definition in section 2(x) of the DPDP Act, 2023 has clarified the matter by adding the words "fully or partly automated."

3. Obligations of the data fiduciary for processing

After comparing the important definitions, we now turn our attention to the obligations cast upon the "data fiduciaries" under the DPD Act, 2023, with the objective of protecting the information privacy rights of the individuals.

3.1 Grounds for processing personal data

The section 4 of the DPDP Act, 2023 permits the processing of personal data for a lawful purpose only if the individual concerned (i.e., data principal) has consented to such processing or the processing is for specified legitimate objectives ([1], p. 04).

The articles 5.1 and 5.2 of the Convention 108+ provide that personal data can only be processed for legitimate purpose either on the basis of the consent of the individual or for some other legitimate objectives laid down by law ([5], p. 08).

The article 6.1 of the GDPR lays down that personal data will be processed lawfully only if the concerned individual has consented to such processing or for other specified legitimate purposes ([6], p. L119/36).

The Committee of Experts proposed in clauses 4 and 5 of the PDP Bill, 2018 that personal data can be processed for clear, lawful, and specific purpose, while respecting the privacy of the individual ([2], p. 06).

The JPC recommended in clauses 4 and 5 of the DP Bill, 2021 that personal data shall be processed lawfully for the purpose consented to by the individual or for specified legitimate purposes ([3], p. 09).

The authors find that the sections 4 and 5 of the DPD Act, 2023 adequately provide for protection of personal data by permitting lawful processing only after obtaining consent of the concerned individual or for legitimate purposes laid down in the DPD Act, 2023. This complies with the established data protection principle of purpose limitation.

3.2 Notice to the data principal before processing the data

The section 5(1) of the DPD Act, 2023 requires that every request for obtaining consent of the individual should be accompanied or proceeded by a notice to the individual conveying the information including the purpose for processing and the provisions available to the individual to exercise his/her rights of grievance redressal and making of a complaint to the regulatory body, that is, the Data Protection Board of India ([1], p. 04).

The articles 8.1.b and 8.1.c of the Convention 108+ require the data controller (i.e., the data fiduciary in case of India) to notify the data subject (data principal of India), the legal basis and the purpose of proposed processing, and the mechanism of exercising the rights of the data subject ([5], p. 08).

The articles 13.1. (c) and 13.2. (d) of the GDPR require the data controller (i.e., the data fiduciary of India) to inform the data subject (i.e., the data principal of India), the purpose and legal basis of the processing, and the right of the data subject to lodge a complaint with the supervising authorities ([6], p. L119/40–41).

The Committee of Experts of India proposed in the clause 8(1) of the PDP Bill, 2018 that the data fiduciary is obligated to notify the data principal either before processing or not later than at the time of processing, the lawful purpose of processing, and the information including the procedures for grievance redressal and the approach to the Data Protection Authority ([2], p. 07).

The JPC recommended in clause 7(1) of the D.P. Bill, 2021 that at the time of processing, the data fiduciary shall notify to the data principal the details including the purpose of processing and mechanism for grievance redressal and filing of complaints to the Data Protection Authority ([3], p. 9–10).

The authors find that the contents of section 5 of the DPD Act, 2023 are much shorter as compared to the contents of the corresponding clause 8 of the PDP Bill, 2018 and clause 7 of the DP Bill, 2021. The contexts are much shorter even when compared with the corresponding article 13 of the GDPR. The sketchy nature of the section 5 of the DPD Act, 2023 might prove inadequate on many essential requirements of notice.

3.3 Consent of the individual

Section 6(1) of the DPDP Act, 2023 requires the data fiduciary to ensure that the consent accorded by the data principal is free, informed, and unambiguous and the consent should express an agreement for the proposed processing ([1], p. 05).

The article 5.2 of the Convention 108+ requires that the consent should be free, specific, informed, and unambiguous ([5], p. 08).

The article 7.2 of the G.D.P.R. requires the consent to be clear, in a plain language and not in violation of the Regulation ([6], p. L119/37).

The Committee of Experts proposed in clause 12(2) of the PDP Bill, 2018 that consent should be free (with reference to section 14 of the Indian Contract, Act, 1872), informed, specific, clear, and capable to be withdrawn ([2], p. 09).

The ingredients of a valid consent, recommended by the JPC in clause 11(2) of the DP Bill, 2021 are similar to the ingredients proposed by the Committee of Experts in the clause 12(2) of the PDP Bill 2018 ([3], p. 11–12).

The authors find that the essential conditions for a valid consent of the data principal are adequately provided in the section 6(1) of the DPDP Act, 2023 to obligate the data fiduciary to obtain a free and unambiguous consent. The section 6(2) further strengthens the information privacy right of the individual by prohibiting any consent which is in violation of the DPD Act, 2023 or the rules made thereunder or any other law of India ([1], p. 05).

The section 6(3) of the Act permits the data principal the option to give his consent in English or in any of the languages listed in the eighth Schedule of the Constitution of India ([1], p. 05). Further, under the section 6(4) of the Act, the data principal is entitled to withdraw his consent ([1], p. 05).

However, one red flag is apparent in the section 6(5), which requires the individual to bear the consequences of withdrawal of consent ([1], p. 05). A provision of liability of individual was proposed by the JPC in clause 11(6) of the DP Bill, 2021, which makes the data principal liable to bear the consequences, if the consent is withdrawn without any valid reason ([3], p. 12). Neither the Convention 108+ nor the GDPR put such a liability on the individual for the withdrawal of consent.

The Committee of Experts had proposed a liability on the individual in clause 12(5) of the PDP Bill, 2018 when the data principal withdraws the consent for the processing that is necessary for the performance of a contract to which the data principal is a party ([2], p. 09). The Committee of Experts was of the opinion that if the withdrawal of consent hinders the performance of a contract, then the data principal could choose to face the specific consequences that flow from the non-performance of the contract ([7], p. 42).

The authors find that the language of subsection (5) of section 6 of the DPDP Act, 2023 leaves scope for any unjustified liability on the individual, unless the subsection is amended to specify that consequences would mean the consequences of hindrance in the performance of a contract, in which the data principal is a party.

3.4 Absolute obligation of the data fiduciary

The section 8(1) of the DPD Act, 2023 makes the data fiduciary liable for complying with the Act, even if the processing is done on its behalf by any data processor ([1], p. 07).

The Convention 108+ does not cast such an absolute liability on the controller (i.e., the data fiduciary), but the articles 28.1 and 28.2 of the GDPR entrust the responsibility on the controller (i.e., data fiduciary) to ensure that the processing meets the requirements of the Regulation and that the data processor cannot engage another data processor without obtaining the specific authorization of the data controller ([6], p. L119/49).

The Committee of Experts was of the view that the liability of the data processor may differ from the liability of a data fiduciary and so the required due diligence needs to be incorporated in the contract, to be signed between the fiduciary and the processor ([7], p. 52). The Committee, further, proposed in the clause 11 of the PDP Bill, 2018 that the data fiduciary would be liable for compliance even if the processing is done by the processor employed by the data fiduciary ([2], p. 11).

The JPC recommended a similar provision in clause 10 of the DP Bill, 2021 by making data fiduciary liable for complying with the provisions of the law in respect of the processing undertaken on its behalf ([3], p. 11).

The authors find the section 8(1) an appropriately worded section that rightfully makes the data fiduciary absolutely accountable, considering that the relationship between the fiduciary and the data principal is not a contract, between two equal parties.

3.5 Obligation of maintenance of data quality

Section 8(3) of the DPDP Act, 2023 requires a data fiduciary to maintain the accuracy, completeness, and consistency while processing any personal data ([1], p. 07). This is a widely accepted principle of data quality. The article 5.4.d of the Convention 108+ mandates that the personal data being processed should be accurate and updated ([5], p. 08). The article 5.1. (d) of the GDPR requires the personal data to be accurate, updated, and for this the inaccurate data should be erased or rectified without delay ([6], p. L119/35).

The Committee of Experts proposed in clause 9(1) of the PDP Bill, 2018 that the data fiduciary shall ensure that the personal data processed is accurate, complete, updated, and not misleading ([2], p. 08).

The JPC recommended a provision [similar to the clause 9(1) of the PDP Bill, 2019] in clause 8(1), mandating the data fiduciary to ensure that the personal data processed is accurate updated, complete, and not misleading ([3], p. 10).

The authors find that the principle of data quality is well articulated in the section 8(3) of the DPDP Act, 2023.

3.6 Limitations on retention of personal data

The section 8(7) of the DPD Act, 2023 obligates the data fiduciary to erase the personal data after its purpose has been served or after the individual has withdrawn the consent ([1], p. 7–8).

The article 5.3.e point of the Convention 108+ prohibits the retention of personal data once the purpose for processing the data is no longer served ([5], p. 08).

The article 5.1. (e) of the GDPR permits the processing of personal data only for the time period for which processing is necessary ([6], p. L119/36).

The Committee of Experts proposed in clause 10(1) of the PDP Bill, 2018 that retention of personal data is permitted only till the time the purpose of processing is served ([2], p. 08). However, the subclause (2) of the clause 10 of the PDP Bill, 2018 permits the retention for longer period if such retention is specifically mandated for complying with any law ([2], p. 08).

The JPC recommended the data retention provision in clause 9(1) of the DP Bill, 2021 by prohibiting the retention of personal data beyond the period necessary to achieve the purpose of processing and require the data fiduciary to delete the data at the end of that period ([3], p. 11). Further, the clause 9(2) of the DP Bill, 2021 permits retention beyond the period if specifically consented to by the data principal or if it is necessary to comply with any law ([3], p. 11).

The authors find that the data retention limitation principle has been appropriately incorporated in the section 8(7) of the DPDP Act, 2023. This section has demonstrated that the chapter II of the DPDP Act, 2023 lays down substantial obligations on the data fiduciaries and the data processors to achieve the objective of protecting the information privacy rights of the individual. In the next section, we will evaluate the provisions of the data protection rights stipulated in the chapter III of the DPDP Act, 2023.

4. Data protection rights of the individuals

The rights based on the personal data protection principles that evolved globally have been incorporated in the DPDP Act, 2023. These rights are now being examined beginning with the section 11.

4.1 Right of the individual to access his/her personal information

Section 11 of the DPDP Act, 2023 provides to the individual the right to obtain information about his/her personal data from the data fiduciary. The information includes the personal data that is being processed, the details of the data processors and other data fiduciaries with whom the personal data is being shared, and the personal data already shared ([1], p. 09).

The article 9.1.b of Convention 108+ of the Council of Europe provides that the individual has a right to obtain without excessive delay or expenses the confirmation of processing of his/her personal data ([5], p. 09). The information to be obtained in an intelligible form includes the data processed, the origin of the data, the retention period of the data, and the steps taken by the data controller to ensure transparency of processing ([5], p. 09).

The article 15 of the GDPR of the European Union provides the data subject (i.e., the data principal of India) the right to obtain information from the data controller including the purpose of processing the categories or personal data processed, the recipients of the personal data, the retention period of data, the origin of the data, and the automated decision making ([6], p. L119/43). Further, the individual has the right under the article 15 of the GDPR to obtain one copy free of cost of the personal data, which is being processed ([6], p. L119/43).

The Committee of Experts of India proposed in clause 24(1) of the PDP Bill, 2018 the right of the data principal to obtain information on the personal data including the personal data being processed or has been processed, the processing activities conducted, and the notice that was required to be furnished to the data principal ([2], p. 14). The clause 24(2) of the PDP Bill, 2018 mandates the data fiduciary to furnish information in a form that is easily understood by a reasonable person ([2], p. 14).

The JPC in clause 17(1) and (2) of the DP Bill, 2021 recommended the right to access and confirmation with the language similar to the contents of article 24(1) and (2) of the PDP Bill, 2018 ([3], p. 16).

The authors find that the right of access has been appropriately incorporated in the DPDP Bill, 2023.

4.2 Right to correction and erasure of personal data

The section 12(1) of the DPDP Act, 2023 confers on the individual, the right to correction and erasure of the personal data ([1], p. 10). The section 12(2) requires that on receiving the request of the data principal, the data fiduciary will make the requested correction, updation, or erasure ([1], p. 10).

The article 9.1.e of the Convention 108+ provides that an individual's request for erasure or rectification will be attended to and the action of rectification/erasure will be communicated to the individual if the processing had been done contrary to the provisions of Convention 108+ ([5], p. 9).

The article 16 of the GDPR confers on the individual, the right to rectification, and erasure of personal data ([6], p. L119/43). The article 17 mandates that the data controller shall, without undue delay, erase the personal data relating to the individual (data principal of India) ([6], p. L119/43).

The Committee of Experts proposed in the clause 25(1) of the PDP Bill, 2018 that the data fiduciary is required to correct, complete, and update the personal data on a request made by the individual ([2], p. 14–15). The clause 25(4) proposed that the data shall take all reasonable steps to notify all relevant entities that the data erasure or rectification or updation has taken place ([2], p. 15).

The JPC recommended in clause 18 of the DP Bill, 2021 the right to erasure and rectification on the lines of the clause 25 of the PDP Bill, 2018 ([3], p. 17).

The authors find that the provisions of subsections (1) and (2) of the section 12 of the DPDP Act, 2023 are adequate for listing the right of correction, updation, and erasure of personal data of the individual (i.e., data principal).

However, subsection (3) of the section 12 of the Act provides for an exception from erasure, in the circumstances when the data fiduciary finds the retention necessary for any particular purpose or for the compliance of any law ([1], p. 10).

4.3 Right to grievance redressal

The section 13 of the DPDP Act, 2023 mandates the data fiduciary to address the grievance of the individual. The section 13(1) of the Act confers a right on the data principal to avail the grievance redressal mechanism provided by the data fiduciary in relation to the obligation cast upon the data fiduciary in respect to the personal data or in relation to the exercise of the right of the data principal ([1], p. 10). The section 13(2) requires the data fiduciary to respond to the grievance within the prescribed time limit ([1], p. 10).

The article 9.1.f of the Convention 108+ confers the right on the data fiduciary to a remedy under article 12 when the rights guaranteed under the Convention are infringed ([5], p. 9). The article 12 of the Convention 108+ mandates each member of the Convention 108+ to provide for judicial as well as non-judicial sanctions and remedies for infringement of the provisions of the Convention ([5], p. 10).

The article 77(1) of the GDPR confers a right on the individual to lodge a complaint to the supervisory authority if the processing of personal data violates the Regulation ([6], p. L119/80). The subarticle (2) of the article 77, further, requires the supervisory authority to inform the complainant about the action taken on the complaint ([6], p. L119/80). The article 78(2) of the GDPR guarantees to the individual the right to an effective judicial remedy where the supervisory authority does not address the complaint or does not respond within 3 months of the lodging of complaint ([6], p. L119/80). The article 79 of the GDPR provides that proceedings against the data controller (data fiduciary of India) and data processor shall be entertained by the Courts of the member State where the controller or processor has an establishment or the Courts of the member State where the individual has his or her habitual residence ([6], p. L119/80).

The Committee of Experts of India proposed in clause 39(3) that any grievance raised by the data principal shall be resolved by the data fiduciary within 30 days of the registering of grievance ([2], p. 23). The clause 39(4) of the PDP Bill, 2018 provides to the data principal a right to file a complaint with the adjudicating authority if the data principal is not satisfied with the handling of the grievance by the data fiduciary ([2], p. 23). The clause 39(5) of the Bill provided for filing of appeal with the Appellate Tribunal against the decision of the Adjudicating Authority ([2], p. 23).

The JPC recommended in clause 32 (2) of the DP Bill, 2021 the provision of a complaint by the data principal to the data fiduciary [3]. In clauses 32(3) and 32(5), the JPC proposed the provision of a complaint to the Adjudicating Authority, on the lines of the PDP Bill, 2018 ([3], p. 28). In clause 68(1)(d) of the DP Bill, 2021, the JPC provided the provision of appeal to the Appellate Tribunal against the decision of the Adjudicating Authority ([3], p. 51).

The section 27(1)(b) of the DPDP Act, 2023, provides the mechanism of a complaint to be filed by the individual, that is, the data principal, to the Data Protection Board of India against the data fiduciary when the data fiduciary fails to satisfy that the rights of the data principal are protected ([1], p. 14). The section 29(1) of the Act provides for the filing of an appeal before the Appellate Tribunal, if the individual (including the data principal) is aggrieved by the decision of the Adjudicating Authority of the Data Protection Board of India ([1], p. 15).

The authors conclude that the provision of grievance redressal against the data fiduciary and the Data Protection Board is adequately and appropriately incorporated in the DPDP Act, 2023.

4.4 Rights to nominate

The section 14(1) of the DPDP Act, 2023 confers on the data principal, the right to nominate a representative (nominee) who can exercise the rights of the data principal in the event of death or incapability of the data principal ([1], p. 10).

The Convention 108+ does not have any provision for a nomination similar to the nomination under section 14(1) of the DPDP Act, 2023.

However, the article 80 of the GDPR provides the data principal, the right to nominate, an organization working in the field of protection or personal data, on his or her behalf and to exercise the right of data protection on his or her behalf ([6], p. L119/81).

4.5 Amendment to the RTI Act, 2005

The section 44(3) of the DPDP Act, 2023 substitutes a smaller provision in the section 8(1) (j) of the Right to Information act, 2005 ([1], p. 20). This provision of the DPDP Act, 2023 has significantly enhanced the protection of privacy of the individuals whose personal information is sought under the provision of RTI Act, 2005.

The authors find that with this provision, the right to information privacy will be strengthened *vis a vis* the right to information under the RTI Act, 2005.

4.6 Absence of a right to data portability

The authors find it strange that the right of the individual to obtain the personal data in the format comprehended by him/her is absent from the DPDP Act, 2023.

Although the Convention 108+ does not have any provision of right of data portability, the article 20.1 of the GDPR provides that the individual (the data subject) shall have the right to receive the personal data in a commonly used and machine readable format ([6], p. L119/45).

The Committee of Experts of India had proposed in clause 26 of the PDP Bill, 2018, a right to the data principal to receive the personal data in a structured, commonly used and machine readable format ([2], p. 15).

The JPC recommended in clause 19 of the DP Bill, 2021, the right to data portability, largely on the lines of the language of clause 26 of the PDP Bill, 2018 ([3], p. 27–28).

The authors find it a shortcoming in the DPD Act, 2023 that the right to data portability is not included as a specific section or subsection in the Act, whereas both the expert bodies namely the Committee of Experts headed by Justice B.N. Srikrishna and the Joint Committee of Parliament had dedicated a specific clause on the right to data portability.

4.7 Absence of a right to be forgotten

The authors experience another academic worry over the absence in the DPDP Act, 2023 of a specific clause on the individual's right to be forgotten.

The Convention 108+ does not have any specific provision on the right to be forgotten, but the GDPR has dedicated a full article on the right to be forgotten. The article 17 of the GDPR provides the individuals (i.e., the data subject) the right to be forgotten and the data controller is obligated to erase without undue delay, the personal data in the situations including the ceasing of the necessity of the data for the purpose of processing; the withdrawal of consent by the data principal and the personal data has been unlawfully processed ([6], p. L119/44).

The Committee of Experts had proposed in the clause 27 of the PDP Bill, 2018 a provision of the right to be forgotten, on the lines of the language of the article 17 of the GDPR ([2], p. 16).

The JPC had recommended in clause 20 of the DP Bill, 2021, the individual's right to be forgotten, on the lines of the language of the PDP Bill 2018 ([3], p. 18–19).

The emphasis on the right to be forgotten is prominent in the order dated 24th August, 2017 of Justice S.K. Kaul, in the nine judge bench decision in K.S. Puttaswamy v. Union of India. Justice Kaul is of the view that an individual should be able to change his/her beliefs and evolve as a person ([8], p. 34). Justice Kaul justified the right with the reasoning that an individual should not be made to live with the fear that the views he/she expresses would forever be associated with him/her and so the individual would refrain from expressing himself/herself ([8], p. 34).

The authors are of the opinion that a specific section on the lines of the clauses recommended by the JPC and the Committee of Experts, on the right to be forgotten, would have emphasized the individual's undisputed right over his personal data.

After examining the obligations of the data fiduciaries in Section 3 and the specifically laid down rights of information privacy in the Section 4, we now examine the mechanism of enforcement of the data protection rights under the DPDP Act, 2023.

5. Penal action for violation of the rights of the individuals

In continuation of the right to grievance redressal explained in the paragraph 4.3(supra), we will evaluate the provisions of the Act that relate to action against the violation of the information privacy rights.

5.1 Penalties

The section 33(1) of the DPDP Act, 2023 provides that the Data Protection Board of India (in short being called "the Board") may, after following the principles of natural justice, impose a monetary penalty on the person who has caused the breach of the provisions of the Act ([1], p. 16–17). The schedule appeared to the Act lists the maximum amount of penalty as two hundred and fifty crore rupees ([1], p. 21). The section 34 of the Act mandates that the amount received as penalties would form part of the Consolidated Fund of India ([1], p. 17).

The article 12 of the Convention 108+ mandates the member States to set up the mechanism of judicial as well as non-judicial sanctions and remedies to address the infringement of the provisions of the Convention ([5], p. 10).

The article 84 of the GDPR requires the member States to provide for by law, the penalties to address the infringement of the Regulation ([6], p. L119/83).

The Committee of Experts had proposed in sections 69(1) and 69(2) of the PDP Bill, 2018 a monetary penalty for infringement of the provisions of the Act. The upper limits of the penalty amount was fifteen crore rupees or 4 percent of the worldwide turnover of the data fiduciary, whichever was higher ([2], p. 41–42).

The JPC recommended in the clause 57–61 of the DP Bill, 2021, penalties on the data fiduciaries and data processors for contravention of the provisions of the Act, including violation of the information privacy rights of the individuals. The upper limit of the amount of penalty in the DP Bill was fifteen crore rupees or 4% of the total worldwide turnover of the data fiduciary, whichever was higher ([3], p. 46).

The authors find that the penalties have been appropriately stipulated under section 33 of the DPDP Act, 2023. Prima facie, the upper limit of penalty seems too harsh, but for deterring the violation, exemplary and harsh penalties are appropriate.

5.2 Absence of the provision of compensation

The DPDP Act, 2023 does not have any provision for payment of compensation to the data principals for the harm suffered by them.

While the Convention 108+ does not have any provision for compensation, the article 82 of the GDPR provides a provision of compensation. The article 82(1) of the GDPR mandates that any person who suffers damage (whether material or non-material) due to the violation of the Regulation would have a right to receive the compensation from the data controller or the data processor ([2], p. 44).

The Committee of Experts of India was of the opinion that data principals need to be compensated by the data fiduciary or data processor for the harm caused to the data principal by the violation of the law ([3], p. 165). Thereafter, the Committee of Experts proposed in clause 75 of the PDP Bill, 2018 that the data principal who suffered harm due to the infringement of any provision of law, would have a right to seek compensation from the data fiduciary or the data processor ([2], p. 44).

The JPC in clause 65(1) recommended compensation to a data principal who suffers harm due to the infringement of the provisions of the law of data protection ([3], p. 49).

The authors find that the absence of the provision of compensation for the harm would be a hindrance in the strengthening of the right to privacy. The authors agree with the views of the Committee of Experts and the JPC that compensation for the harm suffered should be a right of the data principal.

5.3 Bar of jurisdiction of the civil court

Section 39 of the DPD Act, 2023 bars the civil courts from any jurisdiction, or any proceeding, or any action for which the Data Protection Board of India is empowered under the Act ([1], p. 18). Further, the section 38(2) of the Act mandates that the provisions of the DPDP Act, 2023 would prevail to the extent of any conflict between the DPDP Act, 2023 and any other law ([1], p. 18).

The Committee of Experts proposed in clause 89 of the PDP Bill, 2018 that civil courts would not have any jurisdiction to entertain any proceeding for which the Appellate Tribunal is empowered under the Act ([2], p. 51). The clause 89 of the Bill, further, bars any civil court or other authority from granting any injunction in respect of any action taken in pursuance of any power or duty conferred by that Act ([2], p. 60). The clause 110 of the PDP Bill, 2018, had proposed an overriding effect to the Data Protection Act over any other law or any instrument having the force of a law ([3], p. 55).

The JPC recommended in clause 78, the exclusion of the jurisdiction of civil court on the lines of the language of the provision of clause 89 of the PDP Bill, 2018 ([3], p. 66). Further, the JPC recommended in clause 97 that the provisions of the law would have overriding effect on the lines of the language of clause 110 of the PDP Bill, 2018.

The authors find that the overriding effect has rightfully been given to the DPD Act, 2023. This strengthens the letter and law to strengthen the right of the individual to information privacy.

6. Enforcement mechanism

It is often said that *a law is as good as its enforcement.* So, the provisions related to the enforcement of the information privacy rights of the data principal will now be discussed. The mechanism of enforcement of the rights is stipulated in the three chapters of the DPD Act, 2023. The chapter V (comprising sections 18 to 26) relates to the establishment of the Data Protection Board of India (hereinafter abbreviated as DPBI). The chapter VI (comprising sections 27 and 28) delineates the powers, functions, and the applicable procedures of the DPBI. The chapter VII (comprising sections 29 to 32) relates to the Appellate and Alternate Dispute Resolution.

6.1 Constitution of the DPBI

The sections 18(1) and 18(2) of the DPDP Act, 2023 provide that the Central Government shall establish a corporate body named as the Data Protection Board of India ([1], p. 12). The subsection (3) of section 19 requires that the persons of ability, integrity, and standing are eligible to be considered for the chairpersonship or membership of the DPBI if they have special knowledge or practical experience in the fields including data governance, consumer protection laws, information technology, digital economy, law, and techno-regulation ([1], p. 12). The subsection (3) of section 19 further mandates that at least one among the members or chairperson of the DPBI shall be an expert of law ([1], p. 12). The subsection (2) of section 20 limits the term of office of the chairperson and member to 2 years and permits their re-appointment ([1], p. 12).

The authors feel that the qualifications stipulated are appropriate but find that the tenure of the chairperson or member should be at least 3 years in order to ensure a reasonable continuity as required under the Administrative law.

6.2 Powers and functions of DPBI

The section 27(1) of the PDP Act, 2023 empowers the DPBI to enquire into the data breaches and impose penalties as provided in the Act ([1], p. 12). The subsection (2) of the section 27 mandates that the DPBI may issue directions to the concerned persons and such persons shall be bound to comply with the directions of the DPBI. The subsection (2) provides that before the issue of any such direction, the concerned person(s) shall be given an opportunity of being heard ([1], p. 12).

The authors find it good that the section 28(1) provides that the DPBI shall function as an independent body and shall strive to work as a digital office ([1], p. 12). The authors further welcome that the DPBI has aptly been conferred, under the section 28(7), the powers vested in a civil court under the code of civil procedure 1908 in matters including summoning and enforcing attendance ([1], p. 15).

The subsection (11) of the section 28 empowers the DPBI to either close the proceedings or proceed to impose penalty ([1], p. 15). For arriving at the amount of penalty, the DPBI is provided indication guidelines under section 33 ([1], p. 16–17).

6.3 Appeal and alternate dispute resolution

The sections 29(1) and (2) provide the person aggrieved with the order or direction of the DPBI the right to file an appeal before the Appellate Tribunal ([1], p. 15). The subsection (4) of the section 29 empowers the Appellate Tribunal to confirm, modify, or set-aside the order appealed against ([1], p. 15). The section 2(a) defines that the Telecom Disputes Settlement and Appellate Tribunal (hereinafter called the TDSAT) established under the Telecom Regulatory Authority of India Act, 1997 will be the Appellate Tribunal under the DPDP Act, 2023 ([1], p. 2).

The authors welcome the provisions of section 31 that empowers the DPBI to opt for mediation for resolution of dispute by a mediator mutually agreed upon by the parties ([1], p. 16).

However, the section 48(1) of the Information Technology Act, 2000 after the amendment in the year 2017, mandates that the TDSAT will be Appellate Tribunal under the IT Act, 2000 also ([4], p. 21). The authors, therefore find that an already adequately burdened TDSAT may not be in a position to dispose off the appeals timely.

The authors find it disturbing that the rules under the DPDP Act have not been framed even after 1 year of the notification of the Act. The Act, therefore, remains unimplemented.

7. Suggestions and conclusion

After conducting an analysis of the important definitions, the obligations of the data fiduciary toward the data principals, the rights of the data principals, and the mechanism of enforcement of rights, the authors suggest the following improvements toward strengthening the information privacy rights of the individuals:

7.1 Suggestions

The authors suggest that the section 6(5) of the DPDP Act may be slightly amended to qualify on the withdrawal of consent by adding that the data principal would face legal consequences arising out of withdrawal of consent if the withdrawal results in non-performance of a contract in which the data principal is a party.

Further, the authors suggest that a specific provision may be added in the Digital Data Protection Act, 2023 with the heading "Right to data portability." On the lines of the provision drafted in clause 26 of the PDP Bill, 2018 and the clause 19 of the DP Bill, 2021, the contents of the clause could be conveying that the data principal will have a right to obtain the personal data about him in a structured, commonly used and machine readable format. A dedicated provision on the portability would sensitize the data ecosystem to take the responsibility of maintaining the data in a structured, commonly used and machine readable format.

The authors suggest the incorporation of a specific provision on "the right to be forgotten" in the DPD Act, 2023 on the lines of the provision proposed by the Committee of Experts in clause 27 of the PDP Bill, 2018 and the provision proposed by the Joint Committee of Parliament in clause 20 of the D.P. Bill, 2021. The incorporation of the right as a specific provision would keep the emphasis on the transitory nature of the personal information.

Further, the authors suggest the incorporation of a provision on compensation to the person who suffered harm due to the violation of the law of data protection. The contents of the provision could be on the lines of the clause 75 of the PDP Bill proposed by the Committee of Experts and the clause 65(1) recommended by the Joint Committee of Parliament.

For timely disposal of the appeals under DPDP Act, 2023, the authors suggest an amendment in the chapter VII of the Act by the addition of a section 29A as follows:

7.2 29A. Constitution of appellate tribunal

The Appellate Tribunal under the Act will be called the Digital Data Protection Tribunal and will comprise of a Chairman and such number of members as prescribed. Provided that, at least one member of the Tribunal shall be an expert in the field of law.

7.3 Conclusion

The authors find that after addressing the shortcomings of liability for withdrawal of consent, absence of the clauses on data portability, absence of the right to be forgotten, and the compensation for harm, the provisions of the Data Protection Bill, 2023 adequately address the privacy protection principles evolved under the regimes of the Convention 108+ of the Council of Europe and the GDPR of the European Union. These principles include the consent framework, data minimization principle, collection limitation principle, retention limitation principles, and the correction and erasure principle. Based upon these principles, the rights of information privacy have except the shortcomings discussed in the Section 6.1 above, been incorporated in the DPD Act, 2023 adequately. The right to privacy is not an absolute right. The nine judge bench of the Supreme Court of India had flagged that the right to privacy is not an absolute right ([8], p. 264). The Apex Court of India elaborated that right to privacy can only be restricted by a law which stipulates a procedure which is fair, just, and reasonable ([8], p. 264). The law restricting privacy has also to meet the threefold requirements of legality, the need for the law, and proportionality establishing a nexus between the objects of the law and the means adopted in the law ([8], p. 264).

The authors thus conclude that the rights of information privacy are largely covered in the DPDP Act, 2023 of India and the four changes suggested in the Section 6.1 above are the only four improvements required on the Digital Personal Data Protection Act, 2023.

Author details

Ajay Kumar Bisht* and Neeruganti Shanmuka Sreenivasulu
West Bengal National University of Juridical Sciences, Kolkata, West Bengal, India

*Address all correspondence to: ajayphd2018@nujs.edu

References

[1] The Digital Personal Data Act. 2023. Available from: www.indiacode.nic.in [Accessed: June 15, 2024]

[2] The Personal Data Protection Bill. 2018. Available from: https://www.meity.gov.in [Accessed: June 15, 2024]

[3] The Report of the Joint Committee of Parliament on the Personal Data Protection Bill. 2019. Available from: https://164.100.47.193 [Accessed: June 15, 2024]

[4] The Information Technology Act. 2000. Available from: www.legislative.gov.in [Accessed: June 15, 2024]

[5] The Convention 108+: Convention for the protection of individuals with regard to the processing of the personal data, (in short called Convention 108+). Available from: www.coe.int [Accessed: June 15, 2024]

[6] Regulation (EU)2016/679 of the European Parliament and the Council. Available from: https://eur-lex.europa.cu/legal [Accessed: June 15, 2024]

[7] A Free and Fair Digital Economy: Protecting Privacy, Empowering Indians. Report of the Committee of Experts under the chairmanship of Justice B.N. Srikrishna, 2018 (also called the Report of the Committee of Experts). Available from: www.meity.gov.in [Accessed: June 15, 2024]

[8] Justice K.S. Puttaswamy v. Union of India, WP(C) 494/2012 order dated Aug. 24. 2017, Supreme Court of India. Available from: https://main.sci.gov.in [Accessed: June 20, 2024]

Chapter 5

One for All in Privacy Law: A Relational View on Privacy Based on the Ethics of Care

Jasmijn Boeken

Abstract

This chapter proposes a transition from an individualistic conception of privacy to a relational perspective, challenging traditional approaches on two main fronts. First, considering privacy as an individual matter constitutes an unequal playing field when it is balanced against communal rights. Second, information shared by one person can significantly impact others. This chapter highlights research on group and relational privacy but emphasizes a need for a theoretical foundation, proposing care ethics as a normative basis for a relational perspective. Caring privacy should entail the following criteria: (1) minimizing what is known about persons, (2) recognizing persons as embedded in relationships, (3) viewing the private-public distinction as a continuum, (4) no distinction between personal and general data, (5) information is contextual, (6) respecting personal space, and (7) everyone has it. The core contribution of the caring perspective of privacy is that a loss of privacy for one is a privacy loss for all.

Keywords: privacy, ethics, feminism, AI, care ethics, group privacy

1. Introduction

> *There was of course no way of knowing whether you were being watched at any given moment. How often, or on what system the Thought Police plugged in on any individual wire was guesswork. It was even conceivable that they watched everybody all the time. But at any rate they could plug in your wire whenever they wanted to. You had to live – did live, in the assumption that every sound you made was overheard, and except in darkness, every movement scrutinised. ([1], pp. 4-5)*

George Orwell's prophecy in his famous book 1984 did not come to him through a prophetic revelation. Surveillance has been a pervasive practice throughout history, used in times of peace and war, targeting both adversaries and allies. Nevertheless, Orwell accurately perceived that things were changing. In the past, surveillance was labor-intensive and focused on specific individuals, whereas contemporary surveillance consists of large-scale, automated operations, aided by artificial intelligence. Tracking cookies can follow your every step online; in the physical world, as in

London, every dweller is captured by the CCTV [2], and government agencies aspire backdoors into encrypted communications [3]. As privacy has become a pressing topic due to technological advancements, there is an increased scholarly interest in conceptualizing this evolving landscape.

Traditional academic literature on privacy is very extensive and challenging to categorize. To provide some clarity, this chapter divides the work on privacy into three approaches: (1) control over information, (2) the right to be let alone, and (3) the reductionist approach. While the reductionist stance argues that common law adequately protects privacy, the other two perspectives have influenced privacy laws in the United States [4, 5] and the European Union [6]. While novel privacy theories are developed, these traditional theories are still important to discuss due to their influence on privacy and data protection laws. This chapter does not provide an exhaustive overview of privacy literature but rather discusses some of the most influential works in order to challenge the individualistic perspective. While providing distinct views on privacy, what these traditional conceptions have in common is their consideration of privacy as an individual matter [7–10]. This individuality is especially prevalent within the “notice and consent” focus of the GDPR. While the notice and consent paradigm has had a significant share of critique regarding people’s ability to understand the complexities of privacy [11, 12], this chapter will mainly focus on the general challenges of treating privacy as a matter of the individual.

This chapter discusses two main challenges for the individual conception of privacy. First, considering privacy as an individual matter constitutes an unequal playing field as it is often balanced against communal rights such as national security [13, 14]. Second, and most important for this chapter, information that one person might consensually give away can have a profound impact on others who did not give such consent [8, 9, 15]. This critique of the individualistic conception of privacy leads to the question of whether privacy as an individual right still fits the current reality of large-scale data collection and its use in AI models. An alternative approach could be to look at privacy as relational instead of individualistic. The question that this chapter will answer is: what might a relational conception of privacy entail? While previous work has been done on the idea of relational privacy and group privacy, these novel conceptions miss the solid theoretical foundation that the traditional conceptions of privacy have within the liberal tradition. This chapter aims to provide a normative foundation of relational privacy by using the ethics of care. The ethics of care is based on a conception of individuals as relational and therefore fits with the evermore networked reality of current society [16].

This chapter will first define assessment criteria for a conception of privacy, followed by discussing the three traditional perspectives and assessing their appropriateness. The subsequent section debates, in more detail than the introduction, why the individualistic view on privacy is problematic. This is followed by an overview of alternative ideas on privacy, such as group privacy and relational privacy. Finally, care ethics is introduced, and a caring approach to privacy is proposed.

2. Individualistic conceptions of privacy

In 1970, Westin observed that it is remarkable that a concept as important as privacy has been so poorly theorized. Since then, a lot of scholarly work on privacy has emerged. This section will set forth four conditions that a conception of privacy must meet. The preceding sections will discuss the three traditional perspectives on privacy and assess their usability.

Parker [17] suggests that a definition of privacy should meet three criteria: (1) it must fit the data, (2) it must be simple, and (3) it must be applicable in the courtroom. Gavison [18] adds that the concept of privacy should be value-neutral, because otherwise, it would be too difficult to identify a loss of privacy. While agreeing that neutrality is important in defining a concept, I also want to emphasize that absolute neutrality is impossible. The fourth condition that a conception of privacy should meet, therefore, is to endeavor neutrality. Massing this together, a definition of privacy should be fitting, simple, useful, and endeavor neutrality.

The subsequent sections will discuss three different conceptions of privacy and some of the authors that contributed to this broad field of literature. These conceptions will be put against the four criteria that a definition of privacy should meet as described above. What must be considered is that times have changed significantly since many of the definitions below have been developed. While they thus might have met the criteria before, they could fail to do so in the light of new technological developments.

2.1 Control over information

Westin [19] is the most prominent author of the conception of privacy as having control over information, which constitutes the dominant view in current privacy law and aligns with the broader liberal paradigm [6]. This section will discuss the work of Westin and scholars influenced by Westin. Following this exploration, the applicability of the four criteria for a definition of privacy will be assessed.

Westin famously described privacy as "the claim of individuals, groups, or institutions to determine for themselves when, how, and to what extent information about them is communicated to others" ([19], p. 7). The key element in this conception of privacy is thus the control that people have over information, not only including things like wiretapping but also, for example, personality tests, and thereby it protects the privacy of inner thoughts [19]. The notice and consent paradigm within the GDPR is based on the idea of having control over information [6]. In every step, the consumer gets the option to agree or disagree with the privacy policies and is therefore able to exercise control. Building on this idea of privacy as control, other authors argue to shift focus from control to meaningful choice, which includes the ability of people to make decisions [6, 20]. Companies that incentivize consumers to share information about themselves do not contribute to this ability. This adapted version of Westin's definition thus conceptualizes privacy as not only having control but also having the necessary tools to control personal information.

Parker [17], focusing mainly on the physical realm, defines privacy as control over when and by whom the various parts of us can be sensed. By "sensed," Parker means: "seen, heard, touched, smelled, or tasted" ([17], p. 281). While this definition does not account for the disclosure of personal information, one's thoughts, and psychological state of mind due to its strong focus on the physical [17], it does provide an important insight, as privacy could indeed be a very physical thing. Someone watching you or sitting closely to you so they can smell you is, according to Parker, a violation of privacy.

Nissenbaum's [21] explanation of privacy as contextual integrity is also related to Westin's view of privacy as controlling information, as it is phrased in similar terminology [22]. According to Nissenbaum [21], what constitutes adequate protection of privacy depends on the norms of the context you are in. Nissenbaum's theory is inspired by Walzer's work on spheres of justice. While it might not be an invasion of privacy to provide your doctor with your medical history, when this information is taken outside the medical sphere and provided to your boss in the sphere of labor, it becomes a privacy violation. This focus on privacy as contextual is an important contribution to the academic debate. However, Nissenbaum's work also received critique, as norms are not always easily identified and might quickly change [23].

While acknowledging the distinctions, proponents of the conception of privacy as control identify a loss of privacy as a loss of control, which is the basis of current privacy law. This is also what constitutes the main critique—one also loses privacy when voluntarily sharing information, however, the question is whether this is bad or not [18]. This underscores how this definition of privacy does not meet the criteria of neutrality. Moreover, the relationality of data renders the focus on individuals problematic, as controlling information in the current technological reality is impossible [24–26]. Consequently, while providing important insights, this definition does not fit the data.

2.2 The right to be let alone

This section describes privacy as the right to be let alone, which has its foundations in privacy law in the United States [4]. It will first introduce the work of those some consider the most important authors in the field of privacy: Warren and Brandeis [27]. After delving into their theory, the conception of privacy by Gavison [18] will be discussed, which builds on this idea of privacy as being let alone. This is followed by a discussion based on the four criteria as previously outlined.

Warren and Brandeis [27] contended that the advent of technological innovations in photography and printed newspapers necessitated the formal recognition of the right to privacy. This right to privacy as being let alone was envisioned to protect individuals from having their picture taken without consent or having their private life exposed in the newspaper [27]. Warren and Brandeis define the right to privacy in the following way: "In general, then, the matters of which the publication should be repressed may be described as those which concern the private life, habits, acts, and relations of an individual" ([27], p. 216). In essence, privacy as the right to be let alone thus means that no one should have unauthorized access to you when you are in the private sphere.

Gavison [18] critiques the conception of privacy as proposed by Warren and Brandeis, arguing that their definition of privacy as a negative right, where the government is prohibited to spy on its citizens, falls short. The right to privacy, Gavison contends, should encompass both negative and positive rights, emphasizing the state's duty to protect its citizens against intrusion by other citizens or companies [18]. Proposing an alternative conceptualization, Gavison suggests framing privacy as limited access, containing three core elements: secrecy, anonymity, and access. Secrecy pertains to information known about a person, anonymity is compromised when someone pays attention to you, and access means physical proximity. Gavison thus elevates the concept of privacy as the right to be let alone to a more detailed conception of privacy as limited access.

Whereas the definition as posed by Warren and Brandeis [27] has received substantial criticism for being both too narrow [28] and too broad [29], Gavison [18] gives the conception of privacy as being let alone more substance. Gavison's conception is simple and useful and seems to withhold from giving a normative evaluation.

However, it is a highly individualized view on privacy and does not recognize that when a person is being watched, this might not only affect this one person but could also reveal information about those in proximity or those belonging to the same group, it therefore does not meet the criteria of fitting the data. Gavison's argument that privacy is also a positive right, as well as the attention for secrecy, anonymity, and access, however, should be considered important insights.

2.3 Reductionist approach

The final traditional conception of privacy to discuss is the reductionist approach. The reductionist approach is based on a critique against the other conceptions of privacy as described in the previous sections. What is central to this approach is that the authors contend that we do not need new laws to protect privacy, as it is sufficiently protected within common law.

Thomson emerges as an important critic of the conception of privacy as the right to be let alone, asking: "where is this to end? Is every violation of a right a violation of the right to privacy?" ([28], p. 295). Thomson contends that when a right to privacy seems to be violated, some other rights have been violated as well. For instance, when security agencies spy on a married couple having a quiet fight inside their home, their right to privacy has not been violated, but their right over the person has been violated, which includes the right not to be listened to [28]. Similarly, Posner [30] takes an economic approach, arguing that while privacy can be useful for innovation, further protection will not be fruitful. According to these authors, privacy is thus sufficiently protected within common law.

Gavison [18] criticizes this reductionist approach to privacy, arguing that while other rights might simultaneously be harmed when a loss of privacy occurs, the loss of privacy remains important in itself. The plead made by the reductionist theorists leaves the doors wide open to dismiss any claim of a right to privacy. As Fried [31] notes, this work is inspired by scholars like Friedrich Hayek and Robert Nozick who maintain a hierarchy of rights where privacy is less important than other rights. Furthermore, the fast development of the digital world has changed the issues of privacy significantly, rendering it highly questionable whether the common law would still suffice in protecting it. As the reductionist approach, thus does not really propose a conception of privacy as they argue that this is not necessary, it is not entirely possible to assess it on the four criteria a definition should meet. However, there are indications that this approach does not endeavor neutrality and is a misfit with the data.

3. Challenging individualistic conceptions of privacy

Studying the traditional conceptions of privacy reveals that it is a contested concept. While the three discussed approaches highlight vastly different aspects of privacy, a common thread among them is the perspective of persons as individual atoms [7, 8]. This individualistic viewpoint is not only prevalent within academic literature, it is also the dominant perspective within EU and US privacy laws [5, 32, 33]. This section aims to scrutinize the individualistic perspective on privacy and assert its problematic nature. This entails reflecting on two issues as established in the introduction: individual versus communitarian rights and the fast development of aggregated data and the use of AI technologies.

The individualistic perspective on privacy renders it vulnerable to a communitarian critique, particularly as outlined by Etzioni [34], who argues that the individual right to privacy often takes precedent over the common good while it should instead be balanced. While this statement is contested by Cohen [13] who observes that privacy is often on the losing side of this balancing game, let us discuss Etzioni's argument shortly. Two important cases that Etzioni takes as example are those of testing infants for HIV, where the mother's privacy is put against public health, and the case of registering sex offenders, where the privacy of the offender is put against public safety. Etzioni, in these cases, argues that the common good should take precedence over the individual's right to privacy. While Etzioni's work is a highly valuable contribution to the discussion on privacy, I want to contest the idea of balancing privacy as an individual right against the common good. One possible solution might be to see privacy as important for the common good, while my analysis is not broad enough to argue it would change the outcomes of the two cases, what it would surely do is create an equal playing field. Other authors have also argued in this direction, for example, in favor of seeing privacy as an (aggregate) public good [5, 32], or as a collective value [35, 36]. Both Sætra's [5] and Regan's [36] argument is based on the idea that the privacy decisions of one person influences the privacy of others.

The idea that privacy decisions of one person have an effect that transcends beyond the individual is strengthened by the technological advancements of AI and data aggregation. The second vulnerability of the individualistic view on privacy is thus that it is no longer in line with our technological reality [33]. Especially the harvesting of data on an enormous scale poses a significant challenge to conceptualizing privacy as a matter of the individual [8, 9, 15, 32, 33, 37]. An example of consequences of the rapid harvesting and accumulation of data can be found in new AI models, which show how privacy is no longer an individual decision [33]. For AI, our data is not about an individual, but rather it categorizes us in groups; you can belong to numerous groups based on your gender, sexuality, occupation, age, race, and many more [8]. Whenever you accept tracking cookies, this thus does not only reveal something about you, it reveals something about the groups you belong to, and every person in them. Barocas and Nissenbaum [15] call this the "tyranny of the minority" as few people consenting to a privacy loss affect the privacy of everyone else. Or in other words: "*everyone's privacy depends on what others do*" ([38], p. 558). Barocas and levy [38] explore the concept of privacy dependencies, which can be tie-based, where an observer gains information of someone because the ties they have with someone else. They can also be similarity-based or difference-based, where due to similarities or differences in known attributes, other information can be inferred [38].

In their study, Barocas and Nissenbaum [15] provide multiple examples on how the tyranny of the minority works, which also shows the relationality of data. Jernigan and Mistree [39] show how sexual orientation can be inferred from Facebook profiles, and a study on Rice University alumni reveals that sharing personal details by only 20% of a group allows accurate inference of over 80% [40]. Furthermore, Duhigg's [41] research on Target's advertising strategy demonstrates how a fraction of pregnant women disclosing information affects all pregnant individuals shopping there, in one case leading to the unintended consequence of revealing a teen pregnancy to family members. These examples emphasize that privacy is not solely an individual matter, and the introduction of sophisticated AI systems using aggregated data will ever more correctly infer information about individuals that did not give consent [23]. What makes aggregated data even more problematic is that data accumulates across time and across different sources [32]. The younger the child that enters the internet, the more data will be collected of them over a lifetime.

This section argued that seeing privacy as individualistic creates an unequal playing field when it is balanced against the common good, and that it no longer fits with our technological reality. The issue of tyranny of minority [15] shows how the decisions of an individual regarding their privacy have a profound impact on everyone's privacy. The next section will discuss an alternative way of viewing privacy, transforming it from individualistic to relational.

4. Group privacy

One form of privacy which does not only consider the individual is group privacy [9]. While the GDPR does not mention group privacy [8], it has been mentioned in academic literature and surprisingly even in the famous work of Westin [19]. The more recent work that this section discusses considers group privacy especially due to AI's capability to categorize data subjects into groups, based on our characteristics, like age or nationality, or behavior.

In the renowned work on privacy as control over information, Westin [19] acknowledges the need for group privacy in society. Specifically mentioning the intimate family and the community as important groups. To illustrate this point, Westin proposes that communities might have certain traditions which they would like to keep a private matter of the group. A recurring example in Westin's work regards the idea that personality tests may inadvertently lead to a standard personality based on the white men, potentially disadvantaging minority groups. While Westin offers valuable insights into the significance of privacy for groups, this regrettably does not lead to a broader conception of privacy.

Substantial early work on the topic of group privacy was done by Bloustein [42], who does not consider it as an alternative to individualistic privacy but rather as additional to the right to be let alone: "The right to be let alone protects the integrity and the dignity of the individual. The right to associate with others in confidence – the right of privacy in one's associations – assures the success and integrity of the group purpose" ([42], p. 181). Bloustein sees the group as a collection of individuals, not as a separate entity and discusses examples like the lawyer-client relationship where information is shared that should be kept private. In line with this, Bygrave and Schartum [43] consider the option of collective consent, where established groups can control their consent to data collection in a more organized way.

Further important work on group privacy is done by Floridi [9], who argues that in the digital realm, people are often not considered as individuals but as members of a group—regnant women, people living in Amsterdam, parents, or owners of a particular car. While group data has often been said to be anonymous, accumulating such data can lead back to an individual, as you are part of many groups [9, 15, 33, 44]. Anonymization of data thus is no guarantee for privacy. This leads Floridi to argue that "An ethics addressing each of us as if we were all special Moby-Dicks may be flattering and perhaps, in other respects, not entirely mistaken, but needs to be urgently upgraded. Sometimes the only way to protect a person is to protect the group to which that person belongs" ([9], p. 20).

Influenced by the work of Floridi, Mittelstadt [44] discusses the impact of AI, which creates groups that have no collective identity or agency, providing a complicated legal question on how to protect such group rights. A possible solution according to Mittelstadt is to think of these groups as rightsholders, carrying a moral right to privacy. As these rightsholders cannot be responsible for protecting their own privacy, this should be the task of an organization. Similarly looking into the direction of external organizations for the protection of group privacy, Mantelero [35] suggests this could be done by data protection agencies. This would entail collective data protection by means of risk assessment methods, involving multiple stakeholders to balance the benefit of data collection against the collective data protection rights of groups [35].

Similarly, Loi and Christen [45] worry about AI assembled groups that have no agency. They propose "inferential privacy" to protect us from the inferences made by predictive analytics. Important to mention is that they acknowledge that such predictive analytics can be significantly beneficial for society, as for example showed by the research on increased risk of cancer after smoking [45]. While acknowledging the risks of predictive analytics for privacy, we must not lose sight of the benefits for society. Related to the logic of inferential privacy, Mühlhoff [33] discusses predictive privacy as a concept relevant for protecting both individual and group privacy. Mühlhoff suggests that predictive privacy could protect the community against predictive analytics that could potentially harm society. To effectively reach the goal of predictive privacy, Mühlhoff contends that we need to depart from the liberalist ethics of individualism. Puri [46] argues that privacy exists at multiple levels, both individual as well as of the group. Going further than the discussion on inferential privacy, which focuses on the inferences made by predictive analytics, Puri argues that the process of algorithmic grouping itself is a violation of privacy.

Whereas the view on group privacy as provided by Westin [19], Bloustein [42], and Bygrave and Schartum [43] still holds a very individualistic view of the person. Later work provides a view that is a better fit with current technological reality. Whereas the novel work on group privacy thus overcomes the critique of traditional perspectives of privacy as they do not fit the data, they might be missing the foundation in normative theories that the theories of Westin and Warren and Brandeis have. The individualistic views on privacy are strongly established within liberal theory, providing a solid foundation [6]. Such a foundation in theory would be a valuable contribution to the work of group privacy [46]. Furthermore, the number of groups one is part of is difficult to grasp and is not a static fact [35]. While the work on group privacy thus made valuable contributions to the privacy debate, the static idea of groups might be holding it back. Overcoming this challenge, the subsequent section will discuss relational privacy.

5. Relational privacy

The preceding sections have established that traditional Western views on privacy are based on the individual as atomic entity. While group privacy provides an alternative view, it does not explicitly break with the Western liberal tradition of individuality. Opposed to this Western tradition, cultures such as Indian, Japanese, Buddhist, and Confucian have been posited to adopt a more relational conception of privacy [8]. While the previous sections criticized the individualistic view on privacy in the traditional conceptions, according to Kerr [47] such conceptions already have an implicit relationality in them as they do focus on "the other". However, an explicit view on relational privacy remains necessary. This section will discuss the work that has been done on conceptualizing privacy in a relational way. While not much scholarly work has been devoted to this topic, noteworthy suggestions have been made.

The term "relational privacy" has been used in multiple ways. For example, Sacharoff [48] uses the term to explain that our expectation of privacy is depended on the type of relationship we have. While we do not mind sharing information about our body with our physician, we do mind sharing such information with our boss. Thus, because we make distinctions in what information we share with someone based on the relationship we have with them, Sacharoff considers privacy to be relational. In line with this, Sloan and Warner [49] use relational privacy to describe how we navigate sharing information within different relationships. This must remind us strongly of privacy as contextual integrity from the work of Nissenbaum [21] and is thus susceptible to the same criticism—it is still an individualistic view of privacy. While recognizing the importance of relationships, these conceptions are centered around the individual and thus are not in line with the type of relational privacy this chapter is looking for.

An example of a relational approach to privacy that truly moves away from the individualistic perspective can be found in Ubuntu philosophy, which originates from multiple countries within the African continent [8]. A phrase that is central to Ubuntu philosophy is "Umuntu ngumuntu ngabantu" which can be translated to "a person is a person through other persons" ([8], p. 595). This relational view of the person leads to the conclusion that the protection of privacy should not be up to individuals but should be regulated top-down. This also entails stopping using legal frameworks for privacy that are built on the idea of informed consent [8].

Ma [7] argues for relational privacy based on the ideas from Confucianism, and connects this to views from Western feminist ethics. While there are many different perspectives within Confucianism, the person is generally constituted as situated within a specific environment [7]. The relational perspective on privacy in Confucianism is based on a relational perspective of autonomy [7]. Relational autonomy conceives of autonomy as something that can be learned, a skill that you develop, and this development happens in context of relationships [7]. While Ma does not suggest how privacy law should be established according to this view, the research shows that outside of the Western world there are more relational views on privacy.

A relational view on autonomy can also be found within feminist work, which holds that autonomy is something that can be achieved when social circumstances are supportive of it [50]. Applying such a view of autonomy to privacy, Hargraeves [50] argues that relational privacy should be seen as a "privacy blanket". With such a privacy blanket, privacy can be shared, in the sense that someone can join you under the blanket. Privacy is mobile, it can move from one place to another, leaving behind the strict dichotomy of the private and public spheres. And privacy can be weakened or strengthened [50]. A loss of privacy, in this way, occurs when "our ability to negotiate our level of exposure to or desired level of engagement with those around us" ([50], p. 476) is affected.

Although not being explicitly relational, the work of Marwick and Boyd [10] goes beyond the individual and the group to provide a networked definition of privacy. Studying the privacy experiences of teenagers, they argue that we should see privacy as constituted within relationships and networks [10]. This is a valuable insight that should be elaborated upon, and the focus on relationships will be further discussed in the subsequent section of care ethics as we further shift from an atomic view of the individual toward a relational view.

Whereas the traditional work on privacy as discussed in Section 2 contained the main issue of not fitting the data, a growing body of scholarly work in the fields of group privacy and relational privacy is especially focused on fitting the data.

However, while having its roots in reality and being applicable to novel challenges posed by AI, what these theories lack is a normative basis. This is necessary when it comes to questions of how much privacy there *should* be and when privacy loss is considered *harmful*. The ethics of care is proposed to provide a normative basis for a relational view on privacy [8] and will be discussed in the preceding section.

6. Care ethics

As suggested by the authors on Ubuntu [8] and Confucian [7] ideas on relational privacy, the feminist tradition with its view on the relational person could provide a valuable contribution to the idea of relational privacy. This section will first discuss the complicated relationship between feminism and privacy before introducing the ethics of care and especially its ideas regarding the distinction between the private and public sphere and the relational nature of the person. The goal of this section is to show how the ethics of care could be a useful theoretical foundation for a caring perspective on relational privacy.

Using a feminist theory for a new conception of privacy is an interesting undertaking, as the feminist tradition has been an important critic of the right to privacy [20, 26, 51, 52]. According to early feminist scholarly work, the right to privacy and the division of the public and private sphere have served as legitimization for the oppression of women inside their homes [20, 26, 52]. This resulted in the famous phrase "the personal is political". According to Allen and Mack [53], traditional conceptions of privacy were developed from a position of privilege, ignoring women's perspective on privacy. However, privacy has also been a partner for the feminist tradition, as the right to abortion in the United States relates to the right to privacy [20, 53, 54]. Feminist ethics thus provides a valuable and multifaceted approach to the topic of privacy.

The feminist perspective that this chapter discusses is the ethics of care [55]. Combining the central features of care ethics that Held [56] and Preston and Wickson [57] point out, the five most important features of an ethics of care are that: (1) it recognizes care as a moral value; (2) it values emotions; (3) it considers context; (4) it reconceptualizes the public and private sphere; and (5) it has a relational conception of the person. While all these aspects can provide interesting insights for privacy, this section will limit the discussion to the final two. This will show the great potential of using ethics of care in the debate on privacy, while leaving the details up to future research.

Regarding the distinction between the public and the private sphere, feminist ethics in general and care ethics specifically have had different, but complementary, perspectives. Whereas early feminists argued that the law should be introduced in the domain of the private sphere, the home, care ethics posits that relational care inherent in the private sphere should transcend into the public sphere [58]. In other feminist work, the distinction between the private and public sphere is altogether questioned [16, 50, 53, 59]. Given the evolving technological landscape, it is indeed questionable whether the distinction of spheres is still relevant, as products of firms in the public sphere invade our private homes. The work of Ford [60] provides a valuable contribution as it argues that rather than a dichotomy, the private and public should be seen as a continuum, with private on the one end and public on the other. Whereas this is a good solution to the issue of the public/private divide for now, future work should question whether a divide is necessary altogether or whether the idea of different spheres could be abandoned.

The relational conception of the person as described in care ethics is especially interesting for the relational conception of privacy this chapter is exploring. Care ethics sees the relationships we have with others as what defines us; the caring person is a relational self: "Noticing interdependencies, rather than thinking only or largely in terms of independent individuals and their individual circumstances is one of the central aspects of an ethics of care" ([56], p. 53). A person is not conceived of as a single unit, an atom, but as a being that is embedded within relationships with others [16]. As we are thus embedded within relationships, so is information about us, and so is privacy.

This section discussed the ethics of care as a possible theoretical foundation for a caring, relational conception of privacy. The first key takeaway is that caring for privacy can be applicable to both the private and the public sphere in different degrees, as they constitute a continuum rather than a dichotomy. The second is that we should not see individuals as singular atoms but as constituted within a network of relationships.

7. A caring definition of privacy

This section will propose a caring perspective on privacy, drawing upon all the takeaways from the previous sections. Privacy has been defined in different ways: as a right [27] or as a claim [19], but to make its definition more neutral, I will describe it here as a situation. A situation of privacy can thus be a good thing or a bad thing; sometimes it is necessary to lose some privacy, and sometimes losing privacy is harmful. This section makes a first suggestion of how caring privacy could look like, based on the ethics of care and on all the valuable insights of previous work on privacy.

To have a situation of caring for privacy, the following conditions should be in place:

- What is known about persons is minimized;
- We see persons as embedded in relationships;
- The private and public spheres are seen as a continuum rather than a dichotomy;
- There is no distinction between personal data and general data;
- Information is considered to be contextual;
- Personal space is respected;
- And, everyone has it.

While the first point may come as a surprise, a situation of privacy is not a situation of full seclusion, when nothing is known about a person. It is a situation where what is known is limited to what is strictly necessary for the particular relationship. This relates to the second point, which is that we consider people to be relational; they are not singular atoms; they are networked within relationships. Furthermore, the distinction between the public and private spheres is rephrased, and the distinction between personal data and general data is no longer recognized, as all information can be inferred from aggregating data [23, 33, 61]. Furthermore, as Nissenbaum [21] argued, information is contextual; while sharing certain information in a specific situation may not be a harmful loss of privacy, when this information is taken out of context, the loss might be harmful. Inspired by Gavison's [18] insightful remarks on access and proximity, respect for personal space is also part of a situation of privacy. The final and most important point is that a situation of privacy can only exist as long as everyone has it: a privacy loss for one is a privacy loss for all.

Returning to the criteria a definition of privacy should meet as described in section two, it should be fitting, simple, useful, and endeavor neutrality. Whereas the conceptions of privacy as discussed in Section 2 were problematic in the sense that they did not fit the data, the caring definition of privacy solves this issue by approaching it from a relational perspective. The definition is as simple as possible regarding the difficulty of the topic. It is useful due to its clear imperative that privacy should not be an individual decision but governmental. It endeavors neutrality because to have privacy can be good or bad, and to have a loss of privacy can also be good or bad. It is up to the political community to decide when a loss of privacy is harmful. The caring definition of privacy should be all-encompassing, not only considering informational privacy but also decisional- and physical privacy. While this chapter only slightly lifts the veil of what a caring perspective of privacy has to offer, it clearly shows its potential.

8. Conclusion

> *"We can achieve a sort of control under which the controlled, though they are following a code much more scrupulously than was ever the case under the old system, nevertheless feel free. They are doing what they want to do, not what they are forced to do. That's the source of the tremendous power of positive reinforcement – there's no restraint and no revolt. By a careful cultural design, we control not the final behavior, but the inclination to behave – the motives, the desires, the wishes." ([62], pp. 246-247)*

As many other authors, I started my chapter with a quote from Owell's dystopian book *1984*. However, after the findings of this chapter, it seemed more appropriate to finish with a quote from Skinner's [62] *Walden Two,* where, while having a lot of personal freedom in decision-making, the behavior of the people in this imagined society is slowly modified. While the conceptions of privacy that see it as a personal right were great answers to the threat, as described by Orwell, of a government spying on its people, the situation as described by Skinner provides alternative challenges. These challenges are all too real in our current world, where accumulated data can be used for predicting and influencing consumers behavior or political opinions. Our current technological reality of accumulated data collection and the use of it in AI challenges the conceptions of privacy based on an individualistic perspective and calls for novel approaches to privacy.

This chapter shows how the traditional perspectives on privacy contain an individualistic approach. This individualistic perspective on privacy has also been the dominant paradigm within EU and US privacy law. As well as in the GDPR's focus on notice and consent. This chapter challenges the individual conception of privacy based on two arguments. First, considering privacy as an individual matter constitutes an unequal playing field as it is often balanced against communal rights such as national security. Second, and most important for this chapter, information that one person might consensually give away can have a profound impact on others that did not give such consent. The current paradigm on treating privacy as control over information is thus lacking and is construing a dangerous process of desensitization of societies' value for privacy [24]; a different conceptualization of privacy is therefore urgent.

To provide a first glimpse of what an alternative perspective on privacy could entail, this chapter used the ethics of care as a theoretical basis. While not providing a final definition of caring privacy, this chapter suggests that a situation of caring privacy should entail the following criteria: (1) what is known about persons is minimized; (2) we see persons as embedded in relationships; (3) the private and public spheres are seen as a continuum; (4) there is no distinction between personal data and general data; (5) information is considered to be contextual; (6) personal space is respected; and (7) everyone has it. While not downplaying the other points, the most important contribution of the caring perspective of privacy is that when there is a loss of privacy for one, this affects the privacy of all. Furthermore, while a loss of privacy for one might not be harmful, as sharing information strengthens a particular relationship, it may end up being harmful for others, as the data could be used in predictive models.

What this entails for privacy legislation is that the basis of privacy protection should not be consent of the individual. The government should have an increased role in protecting citizens' privacy. While some might suggest that to give governments this increased power would be undemocratic, I would argue the opposite. As the example of Target [41] showed, within current privacy law, a small group can impact the privacy of all, which is profoundly undemocratic. Governments must change their individualistic perspectives on privacy even though this might in some sense reduce freedom of choice: "People's liberty to dismiss their own privacy is not reduced in order to protect themselves, but in order to prevent them from inflicting harm on others" ([5], p. 8).

As this is a preliminary exploration of combining the ethics of care with the concept of privacy, several topics remain deserving of more attention. These include, but are not limited to; the division between the private and public spheres, the role of emotions in privacy, and the question of what future technological developments could mean for the conception of privacy. Furthermore, the suggestion made by Dourish and Anderson [63] to combine the concepts of privacy and security should be further studied by applying care ethics. Additionally, future scholarly work should further study the ideas on privacy in non-Western philosophy. As this study highlights the valuable ideas from Ubuntu philosophy and Confucianism, there is a lot of work that Western researchers might be overlooking by primarily focusing on Western intellectual heritage.

The right to privacy has been significantly challenged by emerging technologies, and given the early stages of large AI language models at the time of writing, the future might bring even more severe challenges to privacy. Proposing a caring approach to the idea of relational privacy might not seem like a straightforward solution. However, since the individualistic paradigm has reached its expiration date, there is a need for innovative ways of approaching privacy. A caring approach to privacy can overcome the challenges of the individualistic paradigm and provide a solution that fits the data. The future is relational, as a privacy loss for one is a privacy loss for all.

Acknowledgements

This work was funded by NWO (the Dutch Research Council) (grant number NWA.1215.18.008) and is part of the Dutch Research Agenda 2018: *Cyber security – towards a secure and reliable digital domain*.

Author details

Jasmijn Boeken[1,2]

1 Institute of Security and Global Affairs (ISGA), Leiden University, The Hague, The Netherlands

2 Centre of Expertise Cyber Security, The Hague University of Applied Sciences, The Hague, The Netherlands

*Address all correspondence to: j.boeken@fgga.leidenuniv.nl

References

[1] Orwell G. George Orwell 1984. London, UK: Penguin Classics; 2008

[2] Ellis MS. Losing our right to privacy: How far is too far. Birkbeck Law Review. 2014;**2**:173

[3] Lear S. The fight over encryption: Reasons why congress must block the government from compelling technology companies to create backdoors into their devices. Cleveland State Law Review. 2017;**66**:443

[4] Kramer IR. The birth of privacy law: A century since Warren and Brandeis. Catholic University Law Review. 1989;**39**:703

[5] Sætra HS. Privacy as an aggregate public good. Technology in Society. 2020;**63**:101422

[6] Austin LM. Re-reading Westin. Theoretical Inquiries in Law. 2019;**20**:53-81

[7] Ma Y. Relational privacy: Where the east and the west could meet. Proceedings of the Association for Information Science and Technology. 2019;**56**:196-205

[8] Reviglio U, Alunge R. "I am datafied because we are datafied": An Ubuntu perspective on (relational) privacy. Philosophy & Technology. 2020;**33**:595-612

[9] Floridi L. Group privacy: A defence and an interpretation. In: Group Privacy: New Challenges of Data Technologies. Cham: Springer International Publishing AG; 2017. pp. 83-100

[10] Marwick AE, Boyd D. Networked privacy: How teenagers negotiate context in social media. New Media & Society. 2014;**16**:1051-1067

[11] Kröger JL, Lutz OH-M, Ullrich S. The myth of individual control: Mapping the limitations of privacy self-management. 7 Jul 2021. Available at: SSRN 3881776

[12] Solove DJ. Introduction: Privacy self-management and the consent dilemma. Harvard Law Review. 2013;**126**:1880-1903

[13] Cohen JE. What privacy is for. Harvard Law Review. 2012;**126**:1904

[14] Mell P. Big brother at the door: Balancing national security with privacy under the USA PATRIOT act. Denver Law Review. 2002;**80**:375

[15] Barocas S, Nissenbaum H. Big data's end run around anonymity and consent. In: Privacy, Big Data, and the Public Good: Frameworks for Engagement. Vol. 1. New York, NY: Cambridge University Press; 2014. pp. 44-75

[16] Sevenhuijsen S. Citizenship and the Ethics of Care: Feminist Considerations on Justice, Morality and Politics. London: Routledge; 2003

[17] Parker RB. A definition of privacy. Rutgers Law Review. 1973;**27**:275

[18] Gavison R. Privacy and the limits of law. The Yale Law Journal. 1980;**89**:421-471

[19] Westin AF. Privacy and Freedom. New York: Atheneum; 1967

[20] Allen AL. Coercing privacy. William & Mary Law Rev. 1998;**40**:723

[21] Nissenbaum H. Privacy as contextual integrity. Washington Law Review. 2004;**79**:119

[22] Nissenbaum H. Protecting privacy in an information age: The problem

of privacy in public. In: The Ethics of Information Technologies. London: Routledge; 2020. pp. 141-178

[23] Skeba P, Baumer EP. Informational friction as a lens for studying algorithmic aspects of privacy. Proceedings of the ACM on Human-Computer Interaction. 2020;**4**:1-22

[24] Sloan RH, Warner R. Beyond notice and choice: Privacy, norms, and consent. Journal of High Technology Law. 2014;**14**:370

[25] Solove DJ. Conceptualizing privacy. California Law Review. 2002;**90**:1087-1155

[26] Suárez-Gonzalo S. Personal data are political. A feminist view on privacy and big data. Recerca: Revista de pensament i anàlisi. 2019;**24**(2):173-192

[27] Warren SD, Brandeis LD. The right to privacy. Harvard Law Review. 1890;**4**:193-220

[28] Thomson JJ. The right to privacy. Philosophy & Public Affairs. 1975;**4**:295-314

[29] Allen AL. Uneasy Access: Privacy for Women in a Free Society. Totowa, NJ: Rowman & Littlefield; 1988

[30] Posner RA. Privacy, secrecy, and reputation. Buffalo Law Review. 1978;**28**:1

[31] Fried C. Privacy: Economics and ethics: A comment on Posner. Georgia Law Review. 1977;**12**:423

[32] Fairfield JA, Engel C. Privacy as a public good. Duke Law Journal. 2015;**65**:385

[33] Mühlhoff R. Predictive privacy: Collective data protection in the context of artificial intelligence and big data. Big Data & Society. 2023;**10**:20539517231166886

[34] Etzioni A. The Limits of Privacy. New York: Basic Books; 1999

[35] Mantelero A. From group privacy to collective privacy: Towards a new dimension of privacy and data protection in the big data era. In: Group Privacy: New Challenges of Data Technologies. Cham: Springer International Publishing AG; 2017. pp. 139-158

[36] Regan PM. Privacy and the common good: Revisited. In: Social Dimensions of Privacy: Interdisciplinary Perspectives. Cambridge: Cambridge University Press; 2015. pp. 50-70

[37] Taylor L. Safety in Numbers? Group Privacy and Big Data Analytics in the Developing World. Cham: Springer International Publishing AG; 2017

[38] Barocas S, Levy K. Privacy dependencies. Washington Law Review. 2020;**95**:555

[39] Jernigan C, Mistree BF. Gaydar: Facebook friendships expose sexual orientation. First Monday. 2009;**14**(10)

[40] Mislove A, Viswanath B, Gummadi KP. You are who you know: Inferring user profiles in online social networks. In: Proceedings of the Third ACM International Conference on Web Search and Data Mining. 4 Feb 2010. pp. 251-260

[41] Duhigg C. How companies learn your secrets. In: The Best Business Writing 2013. New York: Columbia University Press; 2013. pp. 421-444

[42] Bloustein EJ, Pallone NJ. Individual and group privacy. New York: Routledge; 2019

[43] Bygrave LA, Schartum DW. Consent, proportionality and collective power. In: Reinventing Data Protection? Cham: Springer International Publishing AG; 2009. pp. 157-173

[44] Mittelstadt B. From individual to group privacy in big data analytics. Philosophy & Technology. 2017;**30**:475-494

[45] Loi M, Christen M. Two concepts of group privacy. Philosophy & Technology. 2020;**33**:207-224

[46] Puri A. A theory of group privacy. Cornell Journal of Law and Pub Policy. 2020;**30**:477

[47] Kerr I. Schrödinger's robot: Privacy in uncertain states. Theoretical Inquiries in Law. 2019;**20**:123-154

[48] Sacharoff L. The relational nature of privacy. Lewis & Clark Law Review. 2012;**16**:1249

[49] Sloan RH, Warner R. Relational privacy: Surveillance, common knowledge, and coordination. University of St Thomas Journal of Law & Public Policy. 2017;**11**:1

[50] Hargreaves S. Relational Privacy & Tort. William & Mary Journal of Women & the Law. 2016;**23**:433

[51] Allen A. Unpopular Privacy: What Must we Hide? New York: Oxford University Press; 2011

[52] DeCew JW. The feminist critique of privacy: Past arguments and new social understandings. Social Dimensions of Privacy: Interdisciplinary Perspectives. 2015;**85**:90

[53] Allen AL, Mack E. How privacy got its gender. Northern Illinois University Law Review. 1989;**10**:441

[54] Regan PM. Legislating Privacy: Technology, Social Values, and Public Policy. Chapel Hill: The University of North Carolina Press; 1995

[55] Gary ME. From care ethics to pluralist care theory: The state of the field. Philosophy Compass. 2022;**17**:e12819

[56] Held V. The Ethics of Care: Personal, Political, and Global. New York: Oxford University Press on Demand; 2006

[57] Preston CJ, Wickson F. Broadening the lens for the governance of emerging technologies: Care ethics and agricultural biotechnology. Technology in Society. 2016;**45**:48-57

[58] Ruddick S. Injustice in families: Assault and domination. Justice and Care. 1995;**1995**:203-224

[59] Tronto JC. Caring Democracy: Markets, Equality, and Justice. New York: New York University Press; 2013

[60] Ford SM. Reconceptualizing the public/private distinction in the age of information technology. Information, Communication & Society. 2011;**14**:550-567

[61] Hildebrandt M. Who is profiling who? Invisible visibility. In: Reinventing Data Protection? Cham: Springer International Publishing AG; 2009. pp. 239-252

[62] Skinner BF. Walden two. Indianapolis: Hackett Publishing; 2005

[63] Dourish P, Anderson K. Privacy, security… And risk and danger and secrecy and trust and morality and identity and power: Understanding collective information practices. ISR Technical Report UCI. 2005:1-19. Report No.: UCI-ISR-05-1

Section 2

Data Security Frameworks and Applications

Chapter 6

Enhancing Smart Grid Data Utilization within the Internet of Things Paradigm: A Cyber-Physical Security Framework

Zhijian Hu and Rong Su

Abstract

The integration of Internet of Things (IoT) technologies transforms traditional power systems into smart grids with more opportunities for optimizing power generation and consumption. However, this integration incurs significant cyber-physical security challenges that must be addressed to ensure the authenticity of critical data. This chapter explores the intersection of smart grid data utilization and cyber-physical security within the IoT paradigm. We first introduce the key components of IoT systems and their communication in smart grids, highlighting the interdependencies and vulnerabilities. Then, we discuss the potential risks associated with the collection, transmission, and utilization of data in smart grid environments, emphasizing the importance of cyber-physical security countermeasures in mitigating these risks. Finally, we propose a cyber-physical security framework equipped with dual risk-mitigation layers, including offline parameter configuration and online intrusion detection, to safeguard smart grid data against cyber-physical threats. By adopting this security framework, stakeholders can leverage the full potential of IoT technologies in smart grids while ensuring the security of the critical infrastructure. This chapter contributes to the ongoing discourse on cyber-physical security in smart grids and provides practical insights for policymakers, industry practitioners, and researchers seeking to address the evolving challenges in this domain.

Keywords: internet of things, smart grid, cyber-physical security, data utilization, security framework, risk-mitigation, intrusion detection

1. Introduction

In recent decades, the Internet of Things (IoT) technologies have assumed a pivotal role in the evolution of modern smart grids, significantly enhancing data collection and utilization processes [1]. The integration of IoT technologies provides substantial benefits to smart grids, including advanced smart sensing capabilities and intelligent monitoring systems [2]. However, despite these advantages, the IoT framework presents significant challenges to the secure operation of smart grids.

These challenges arise from both cyber and physical perspectives, particularly in environments characterized by uncertainty. Consequently, addressing these security concerns is crucial to ensuring the reliability and stability of smart grid operations.

The uncertainties originating from the IoT system in smart grids can be broadly categorized into two main aspects: data collection from power infrastructures and devices, and data exchange within IoT communication networks. The first aspect pertains to data collection, which typically involves heterogeneous sensors such as phasor measurement units (PMUs) and remote telemetry units (RTUs). These sensors, often installed in outdoor environments, are composed of numerous intelligent units designed for specific purposes such as data measuring, processing, and broadcasting [3–5]. Due to prolonged exposure to outdoor environments, these sensors face various uncertain factors, including limited processing capacities, functional disorders, sensor aging, and potential physical attacks from adversaries. These limitations can result in temporary sensor failures, leading to the degradation of the authenticity and reliability of the collected data. The second aspect involves data exchange within the IoT communication network. Modern smart grids often span distinct geographical landscapes, including multiple cities and remote communities. These areas share local data with their neighbors in real time, facilitated by wireless sensor networks (WSNs) due to their advantages in flexible deployment, adaptable relocation, and cost-effective installation and maintenance. However, the inherent openness of wireless transmission makes WSNs vulnerable to cyber attacks [6, 7]. Adversaries can exploit these vulnerabilities by injecting false data into the communication links of WSNs, thereby altering data values and potentially destroying the power equipment. These two primary concerns, encompassing both cyber and physical dimensions, form the core topics to be addressed in this chapter.

To address the vulnerabilities inherent in the data collection of smart grids, significant efforts have been undertaken, yielding several promising solutions in recent years [8–15]. For instance, Ref. [8] examined PMU faults from a hardware-software interaction perspective, developing a comprehensive reliability model for PMUs based on Markov models. This model facilitates the estimation of PMU false data using Monte Carlo simulation techniques. Ref. [10] introduced a hybrid algorithm designed for fast path recovery in wide-area measurement systems to mitigate the effects of intermittent PMU outputs. Ref. [11] identified that intermittent PMU measurements are caused by both natural factors and physical attacks. It employed a Bernoulli process with a specified probability to model these intermittent measurements and the degrees of PMU failure. From the perspective of data utilization, various stability criteria have been employed to ensure the efficient operation of smart grids, despite the imperfections in PMU models, such as mean-square asymptotic stability [11] and stochastic stability [13], both of which are essential for guaranteeing the stability and robustness of smart grids amidst imperfect data collection. These methodologies and criteria serve as valuable tools in enhancing the security of smart grids from cyber-physical perspectives, addressing both hardware-software interactions and external threats to data integrity.

In response to cyber attacks targeting data exchange within IoT communication networks, extensive research has been conducted on cyber attack detection methodologies [7, 16]. Prominent methods include intrusion-detector-dependent attack detection [17, 18], credibility-based attack detection [19, 20], observer/filter-based detection [21], and learning-based detection [22]. For instance, Ref. [17] developed a χ^2-detector-dependent approach to identify false data injection (FDI) attacks in distributed frequency regulation, leveraging the decentralized model of each area to provide the frequency reference signal. Ref. [20] incorporated credibility evaluation into frequency regulation within smart grids, effectively mitigating the impact of FDI attacks on frequency dynamics. Ref. [21] proposed a reduced-order observer-based approach for monitoring FDI attacks in large-scale smart grids, utilizing a reduced-order observer to generate residual signals and embedding an adaptive detection threshold to minimize conservativeness. Ref. [7] introduced a data-driven framework encompassing detection, classification, and control signal retrieval to mitigate the impacts of unobservable FDI attacks on smart grids. This framework includes a classifier designed to dynamically learn from historical data and accurately classify FDI attacks under challenging conditions. These advanced methodologies collectively enhance the robustness and security of smart grids against cyber threats, ensuring more reliable operation in the face of unexpected cyber attacks.

Based on the preceding discussion, we acknowledge that these results have contributed to the effective utilization of smart grid data within the IoT architecture. However, these findings are dispersed and lack a unified framework. This chapter aims to establish a comprehensive and systematic framework to enhance smart grid data utilization from both cyber and physical security perspectives, incorporating a wide range of potential uncertainties inherent in the IoT architecture. The proposed framework is designed to be general and represents a significant advancement toward providing a scientific foundation for smart grids in the context of IoT with inherent uncertainties. This framework is inspired from a macro perspective, focusing on system-level data utilization enhancement rather than merely local operations. It is structured into two risk-mitigation layers from cyber-physical perspectives. The first risk-mitigation (physical) layer involves offline control parameter configuration, which aims to integrate easily modeled uncertainties, such as intermittent sensor measurements, into system modeling and control design. This configuration is conducted prior to the deployment of smart grids, thereby contributing to offline security enhancement. To address the inaccurate or incomplete modeling issues that the first layer may not fully resolve, the second risk-mitigation layer is implemented. This layer focuses on online intrusion detection to counter potential cyber attacks within IoT communication networks. The dual-layer framework allows for both independent application and practical integration, providing a high degree of flexibility and universality. This approach offers valuable guidance for both academic researchers and industry practitioners, facilitating effective risk-mitigation and enhancing the reliability of smart grid operations in the face of diverse uncertainties.

The remainder of this chapter is structured as follows. Section 2 introduces the data collection and exchange within IoT in smart grids. Section 3 models the smart grids and potential risks. Section 4 designs the dual-layer security framework for enhancing smart grid data utilization. Section 5 validates the effectiveness of the dual-layer secure framework. Section 6 concludes this chapter.

2. Data collection and exchange within IoT in smart grids

As a representative example of cyber-physical systems, the smart grid exemplifies the intricate interaction between the physical and cyber layers during its operation. The physical layer is primarily responsible for data acquisition, encompassing the measurement and processing of essential signals through various sensor devices, such as PMUs and RTUs. In contrast, the cyber layer focuses on data communication, including the transmission, reception, and exchange of the collected data. Together, these layers form an IoT system, a pivotal concept in the context of smart grids. The IoT system encompasses devices equipped with sensors, computational capabilities, software, and auxiliary technologies, enabling their interconnectivity and data exchange with other devices and systems *via* the Internet or other communication networks. This interconnectivity is crucial for the implementation of supervisory control and data acquisition (SCADA) systems, which monitor the operational states of smart grids. The IoT system's applications span various stages of smart grid operation, including power generation, transmission, distribution, and consumption, thereby enhancing efficiency and reliability [23].

The ways of data exchange within IoT are realized by the communication topology, which is commonly determined by the physical connection. Take a typical application scenario of smart grids, the communication topology of a power generation system is determined by the amount of areas and performance requirements. To better describe the characteristics of the communication topology of smart grids, we here introduce the concept of a directed graph.

In graph theory, $\mathbb{G} = (\mathbb{V}, \mathbb{E}, \mathbb{L})$ represents the mathematical formulation of a directed graph, which is employed to describe the communication topology in this chapter. Here, $\mathbb{V} = \{1, 2, \ldots, n\}$ denotes the set of labels corresponding to different areas. The set $\mathbb{E} \subseteq \mathbb{V} \times \mathbb{V}$ characterizes the communication links between these areas. The adjacency matrix $\mathbb{L} = \left(l_{ij}\right)_{n \times n}$ encodes the presence and weights of these communication links, where $l_{ij} > 0$ indicates that data transmission occurs from the i-th PMU to the j-th PMU. An area j is defined as a neighbor of an area i if $l_{ij} = 1$. Consequently, the set $\mathbb{N}_i \triangleq \{j \in \mathbb{V} | (i,j) \in \mathbb{E}\}$ specifies the neighbors of the i-th PMU, indicating that the i-th PMU can receive state measurements from its neighboring PMUs $j \in \mathbb{N}_i$ according to the defined communication topology.

3. Modeling of smart grids and potential risks

3.1 Modeling of smart grids

This chapter takes the load frequency control (LFC), also named automatic generation control, a typical application in smart grids, as an example. The LFC dynamics of each area contain the following five parts, i.e., generator, governor, power system, tie-line power, and area control error. The dynamics of these five parts are

$$\Delta \dot{P}_{m_i} = -\frac{1}{T_{d_i}} \Delta P_{m_i} + \frac{1}{T_{d_i}} \Delta P_{v_i}, \tag{1}$$

$$\Delta \dot{P}_{v_i} = -\frac{1}{R_i T_{g_i}} \Delta f_i - \frac{1}{T_{g_i}} \Delta P_{v_i} + \frac{1}{T_{g_i}} \Delta P_{c_i}, \tag{2}$$

$$\Delta \dot{f}_i = -\frac{D_i}{T_{m_i}} \Delta f_i + \frac{1}{T_{m_i}} \Delta P_{m_i} - \frac{1}{T_{m_i}} \Delta P^i_{\text{tie}} - \frac{1}{T_{m_i}} \Delta P_{L_i}, \tag{3}$$

$$\Delta \dot{P}^i_{\text{tie}} = \sum_{j=1, j \neq i}^{\mathbb{N}} 2\pi T_{ij} \left(\Delta f_i - \Delta f_j\right), \tag{4}$$

$$ACE_i = \mu_i \Delta f_i + \Delta P^i_{\text{tie}}, \tag{5}$$

Symbol	Physical meaning
Δf_i	deviation of frequency
ΔP_{W_i}	the wind power deviation
ΔP_{m_i}	deviation of generator mechanical power
ΔP_{v_i}	deviation of turbine value position
ΔP^i_{tie}	net tie-line active power flow
ΔP_{L_i}	load disturbance
$\mathbb{N}$	the number of areas
T_{d_i}	time constant of the generator
T_{g_i}	time constant of the governor
T_{m_i}	time constant of the power system
R_i	speed drop
D_i	equivalent damping coefficient of the generator
T_{ij}	tie-line synchronizing coefficient between the area i and j
μ_i	frequency bias constant $\mu_i = 1/R_i + D_i$

Table 1.
Parameters of area i.

where the physical meanings of the system parameters are shown in **Table 1** [11]. The compact form of (1)–(5) can be described as

$$\begin{cases} \dot{x}_i = \mathcal{A}_i x_i + \sum_{j=1, j\neq i}^{\mathbb{N}} \mathcal{A}_{ij} x_j + \mathcal{B}_i u_i + \mathcal{F}_i \omega_i, \\ y_i = \mathcal{C}_i x_i, \end{cases} \tag{6}$$

where $x_i = \begin{bmatrix} \Delta f_i & \Delta P_{m_i} & \Delta P_{v_i} & \Delta P^i_{\text{tie}} & \int ACE_i \end{bmatrix}^T$ denotes the state vector; y_i denotes the measured output; u_i denotes the control input; ω_i denotes the load disturbance;

$$\mathcal{A}_i = \begin{bmatrix} \frac{-D_i}{T_{m_i}} & \frac{1}{T_{m_i}} & 0 & \frac{-1}{T_{m_i}} & 0 \\ 0 & \frac{-1}{T_{d_i}} & \frac{1}{T_{d_i}} & 0 & 0 \\ \frac{-1}{R_i T_{g_i}} & 0 & \frac{-1}{T_{g_i}} & 0 & 0 \\ \sum_{j=1, j\neq i}^{\mathbb{N}} 2\pi T_{ij} & 0 & 0 & 0 & 0 \\ \mu_i & 0 & 0 & 1 & 0 \end{bmatrix},$$

$$\mathcal{A}_{ij} = \begin{bmatrix} 0 & 0 & 0 & 0 & 0 \\ 0 & 0 & 0 & 0 & 0 \\ 0 & 0 & 0 & 0 & 0 \\ -2\pi T_{ij} & 0 & 0 & 0 & 0 \\ 0 & 0 & 0 & 0 & 0 \end{bmatrix}, \ \mathcal{C}_i^T = \begin{bmatrix} \mu_i & 0 \\ 0 & 0 \\ 0 & 0 \\ 1 & 0 \\ 0 & 1 \end{bmatrix},$$
$$\mathcal{B}_i = \begin{bmatrix} 0 & 0 & \frac{1}{T_{g_i}} & 0 & 0 \end{bmatrix}^T, \omega_i = \Delta P_{L_i}, u_i = \Delta P_{c_i},$$
$$\mathcal{F}_i = \begin{bmatrix} \frac{1}{T_{m_i}} & 0 & 0 & 0 & 0 \end{bmatrix}^T. \tag{7}$$

Given that state measurement and feedback control in smart grids are implemented through digital devices like PMUs and RTUs, a discrete-time state-space model is derived to facilitate the subsequent analysis. The discrete-time representation of the continuous-time system model (6) is formulated as

$$\begin{cases} x_i(k+1) = A_i x_i(k) + B_i u_i(k) + \sum\limits_{j=1, j\neq i}^{\mathbb{N}} A_{ij} x_j(k) + F_i \omega_i(k), \\ y_i(k) = C_i x_i(k), \end{cases} \tag{8}$$

where $A_i = e^{\mathcal{A}_i h}$, $B_i = \int_0^h e^{\mathcal{A}_i s} \mathcal{B}_i ds$, $A_{ij} = e^{\mathcal{A}_{ij} h}$, $F_i = \int_0^h e^{\mathcal{A}_i s} \mathcal{F}_i ds$, and $C_i = \mathcal{C}_i$; h denotes the sampling period.

3.2 Potential risks and descriptions

This chapter examines the potential risks to smart grids from both physical and cyber perspectives. Physical risks arise from sensor faults, which can be caused by limited processing capacities, functional impairments, sensor aging, and physical attacks from adversaries. Such sensor faults compromise the authenticity and reliability of the collected data. To model the impact of these physical risks, this chapter utilizes Bernoulli variables to capture the intermittent nature of measurements affected by sensor faults. Consequently, the actual measured output from the sensor i is represented as

$$\bar{y}_i(k) = \theta_i(k) y_i(k), \tag{9}$$

where $\theta_i(k) = 0$ means that the sensor i suffers faults at the time k, while $\theta_i(k) = 1$ means the sensor i is healthy. The probability distribution of $\theta_i(k)$ satisfies

$$\text{Prob}\{\theta_i(k) = 1\} = \bar{\theta}_i, \quad \text{Prob}\{\theta_i(k) = 0\} = 1 - \bar{\theta}_i, \tag{10}$$

where Prob$\{\cdot\}$ denotes the probability operator, $\theta_i(k)$ at different times are assumed to be independent and identically distributed.

Note that $\theta_i(k)$ serves as a comprehensive representation of various factors, including limited processing capacities, functional impairments, sensor aging, and physical attacks from adversaries. Specifically, $\theta_i(k)$ can be expressed as $\theta_i(k) = \theta_i^1(k)\theta_i^2(k)\theta_i^3(k)\cdots\theta_i^M(k)$, where denotes the total number of potential factors contributing to sensor faults.

From the cyber perspective, potential risks arise in the data exchange within the IoT communication network. Modern smart grids typically encompass multiple control areas, which share local data with neighboring areas in real time. However, the inherent openness of these communication networks renders them vulnerable to cyber attacks. Adversaries can inject false data into the communication links based on malicious intent, thereby compromising the data integrity of the national power grid and endangering public safety. In the context of false data injection (FDI) attacks on the communication network, the received data in the control area i, transmitted from neighboring area j, can be modeled as:

$$\tilde{y}_j(k) = \bar{y}_j(k) + G_j g_j(k) \tag{11}$$

where $\bar{y}_j(k)$ denotes the measured output at area j; $g_j(k)$ denotes a column vector implying the false data deliberately injected into the communication link from area j to area i by adversaries; and G_j defines the attack selection matrix. For the purposes of the ensuing sensitivity analysis, G_j is assumed to be a diagonal matrix with entries of 0 or 1, where 0 implies a real measurement and one implies a compromised measurement.

4. Dual-layer security framework for enhancing smart grid data utilization

This chapter endeavors to propose a dual-layer security framework for enhancing smart grid data utilization. Section 4.1 focuses on the first risk-mitigation layer, offline control parameter configuration, while Section 4.2 addresses the second risk-mitigation layer, online intrusion detection. In the following, we will discuss these two layers in detail.

4.1 Offline control parameter configuration: First risk-mitigation layer

Since we focus on multi-area smart grids, the distributed output feedback controller is designed considering the sensor faults, whose mathematical formulation is

$$u_i(k) = \theta_i(k) K_i y_i(k) + \sum_{j=1, j\neq i}^{\mathbb{N}} \theta_j(k) K_{ij} y_j(k), \tag{12}$$

where K_i and K_{ij} are local and neighboring control gains to be determined. Then, the closed-loop system model (8) becomes

$$\begin{cases} x_i(k+1) = (A_i + \theta_i(k) B_i K_i C_i) x_i(k) + \sum\limits_{j=1, j\neq i}^{\mathbb{N}} (A_{ij} + \theta_j(k) B_i K_{ij} C_j) x_j(k) + F_i \omega_i(k), \\ \bar{y}_i(k) = \theta_i(k) C_i x_i(k). \end{cases} \tag{13}$$

Based on the closed-loop system (13), we will propose Theorem 1 and Theorem 2 to facilitate the control parameter configuration.

Theorem 1.1 Considering the sensor fault probability $\overline{\theta}_i$, the closed-loop system (13) is mean-square asymptotically stable with Δf_i satisfying the prescribed $\mathcal{H}_\infty$ performance indicator γ_i if there exist matrices $P_i \succ 0$ such that, for $i = 1, 2, \cdots, \mathbb{N}$,

$$\begin{bmatrix} \Xi + D^T D & \overline{A}^T PF \\ * & F^T PF - \gamma^2 I \end{bmatrix} \prec 0 \tag{14}$$

where P_i is the Lyapunov matrix; "$\succ$" and "$\prec$" define "positive definite" and "negative definite" of a matrix, respectively; " $*$ " denotes the symmetric item of a sophisticated matrix; $\mathrm{Diag}^i_{\mathbb{N}}\{C_i\}$ indicates that only the i-th diagonal block owns a nonzero value C_i while other diagonal blocks are all zero; and
$\Xi = \overline{A}^T P \overline{A} + \sum_{i=1}^{\mathbb{N}} \rho_i^2 L_i^T P L_i - P, \overline{A} = A + BK\overline{\theta}C, B = \mathrm{Diag}\{B_1, B_2, \cdots, B_{\mathbb{N}}\}$,
$C = \mathrm{Diag}\{C_1, C_2, \cdots, C_{\mathbb{N}}\}, D = \mathrm{Diag}\{D_1, D_2, \cdots, D_{\mathbb{N}}\}, F = \mathrm{Diag}\{F_1, F_2, \cdots, F_{\mathbb{N}}\}$,
$P = \mathrm{Diag}\{P_1, P_2, \cdots, P_{\mathbb{N}}\}, \theta = \mathrm{Diag}\{\theta_1, \theta_2, \cdots, \theta_{\mathbb{N}}\}, \gamma = \mathrm{Diag}\{\gamma_1, \gamma_2, \cdots, \gamma_{\mathbb{N}}\}$,
$\overline{\theta} = \mathrm{Diag}\{\overline{\theta}_1, \overline{\theta}_2, \cdots, \overline{\theta}_{\mathbb{N}}\}, \rho_i = \sqrt{\overline{\theta}_i(1 - \overline{\theta}_i)}, D_i = [1\ 0\ 0\ 0\ 0], L_i = BKE_i$,
$E_i = \mathrm{Diag}^i_{\mathbb{N}}\{C_i\}$, A has the identical form with K,

$$K = \begin{bmatrix} K_1 & K_{12} & \cdots & K_{1\mathbb{N}} \\ K_{21} & K_2 & \cdots & K_{2\mathbb{N}} \\ \vdots & \vdots & \ddots & \vdots \\ K_{\mathbb{N}1} & K_{\mathbb{N}2} & \cdots & K_{\mathbb{N}} \end{bmatrix}. \tag{15}$$

Proof: A similar proof procedure can be found in Ref. [24].

Careful readers may observe that condition (14) is not a strict linear matrix inequality (LMI) due to the coupling between the distributed controller gain K and the Lyapunov matrix P. Consequently, to determine the value of K, we further propose Theorem 2.

Theorem 1.2 Considering the sensor fault probability $\overline{\theta}_i$, the closed-loop system (13) is mean-square asymptotically stable with Δf_i satisfying the prescribed $\mathcal{H}_\infty$ performance indicator γ_i if there exist matrices $P_i \succ 0$ and $Q_i \succ 0$ such that, for $i = 1, 2, \cdots, \mathbb{N}$,

$$\begin{bmatrix} -\tilde{Q} & 0 & \overline{L} & 0 \\ * & -Q & \tilde{A} & F \\ * & * & \tilde{D} & 0 \\ * & * & * & -\gamma^2 I \end{bmatrix} \prec 0, \tag{16}$$

$$P_i Q_i = I, \tag{17}$$

where $\tilde{A} = A + BK\overline{\theta}C, \tilde{D} = D^T D - P, \overline{L} = \left[\rho_1 L_1^T(k), \rho_2 L_2^T(k), \cdots, \rho_{\mathbb{N}} L_{\mathbb{N}}^T(k)\right]^T$,
$\tilde{Q} = \mathrm{Diag}_{\mathbb{N}}\{Q, Q, \cdots, Q\}$, and $Q = \mathrm{Diag}\{Q_1, Q_2, \cdots, Q_{\mathbb{N}}\}$.

Proof: A similar proof procedure can be found in Ref. [24].

From Theorem 2, the distributed controller gain K can be determined automatically using the mincx solver in the LMI toolbox. Subsequently, the quantity of the control action can be calculated *via* (12) and applied to update the system (13).

The obtained distributed controller gain K has a certain resiliency to different sensor fault probabilities.

4.2 Online intrusion detection: second risk-mitigation layer

The first risk-mitigation layer aims to tolerate certain categories of easily modeled uncertainties, such as temporary sensor faults, which are modeled offline prior to calculating the controller gains. However, in real-world applications, pre-modeling may be inaccurate or incomplete. Additionally, smart grids may encounter other hard-to-predict uncertainties, such as cyber attacks on communication networks. Consequently, the proposed security framework includes a second risk-mitigation layer to address the deficiencies of the first layer.

To mitigate the impacts of hard-to-predict uncertainties, such as potential false data injection (FDI) attacks on communication networks, on the stable operation of smart grids, an online intrusion detection unit is established at the control center of each area. Given that load disturbances typically follow a normal distribution, this section presents a decentralized model-based χ^2 detection mechanism to evaluate the authenticity of data transmitted from neighboring areas in the presence of potential FDI attacks. This detection unit, installed at the local controller, is responsible for verifying the integrity of received data prior to executing control actions.

The fundamental logic behind χ^2 detection is to identify abnormal signals by comparing the accumulated error between measured values and their estimates against a predefined alarm threshold. The accumulated error is calculated by

$$\xi_j(k) = \sum_{l=k-\Gamma+1}^{k} \left[\hat{y}_j(l) - \tilde{y}_j(l)\right]^T \left[\hat{y}_j(l) - \tilde{y}_j(l)\right], k \geq \Gamma, \tag{18}$$

where $\xi_j(k)$ follows a χ^2 distribution with $5 \times (\Gamma - 1)$ degrees of freedom, $\hat{y}_j(l)$ represents the estimates of neighboring measurements, and Γ denotes the time window used to determine the number of signals considered.

The χ^2 detector at time k is defined as

$$\xi_j(k) \underset{H_1}{\overset{H_0}{\lesseqgtr}} \delta_j \tag{19}$$

where the threshold δ_j is chosen with precision according to the desired security level, Hypothesis H_0 assumes that the received signals are identical to the actual measurements, while the hypothesis H_1 posits that there are significant discrepancies. When hypothesis H_0 is rejected, the hypothesis H_1 is accepted, triggering an alarm. Consequently, the smart grid operators will isolate the compromised communication link.

Note that the precision of the χ^2 detection is tightly related to the selected alarming threshold δ_j. Determining the optimal alarming threshold remains an open challenge in the field. A trade-off is necessary to balance the false isolation rate (FIR), false connection rate (FCR), and average detection time (ADT). The impacts of δ_j on FIR, FCR, and ADT are thoroughly examined through simulations, aiming to provide valuable insights for researchers and practitioners.

In (18), the estimates of neighboring measurements are calculated based on their respective decentralized models, as follows

$$\begin{cases} \hat{x}_j(k+1) = A_j\hat{x}_j(k) + B_ju_j(k), \\ \hat{y}_j(k) = \hat{x}_j(k), \\ \hat{x}_j(0) = \hat{x}_{j0}. \end{cases} \tag{20}$$

where the tie-line related signals in (13) are set as zero in (20), to facilitate the calculation of (18).

4.3 Scalability analysis

Careful readers may observe that the mathematical formulation of each layer in the proposed security framework involves numerous parameters. These parameters significantly influence the framework's implementation efficiency. A particularly important parameter is the subscript i, which appears in almost all mathematical formulas and denotes the number of areas within a large-scale power grid. Theoretically, the number of areas can impact the scalability of the proposed security framework. However, it is advantageous that each area of the large-scale power grid can be represented by an equivalent single-machine-single-load system, ensuring that the number of areas remains manageable. Consequently, each generator within an area will receive a power generation reference based on the reference obtained from the equivalent model and predetermined participation factors. Therefore, scalability is not a concern. The computational complexity and integration cost of the proposed framework with existing systems and control strategies are closely tied to the scale of the smart grid. Given that the number of areas is limited, both computational complexity and integration costs remain reasonable. As a result, the proposed security framework exhibits broad applicability.

5. Validation results

5.1 Structure and parameters of the smart grid

To verify the efficacy of the proposed dual-layer security framework, a four-area fully-connected smart grid is utilized for demonstration. In this configuration, each area is physically interconnected with the other three *via* tie-lines, facilitating mutual communication. The parameters of the smart grid are detailed in **Table 2**.

5.2 First risk-mitigation layer validation

To validate the effectiveness of the first risk-mitigation layer, which involves offline control parameter configuration, a traditional PI controller is used as a benchmark. The traditional controller gains are automatically determined using the LMI toolbox in MATLAB, without accounting for PMU faults. Conversely, the risk-mitigation controller gains are automatically selected using the LMI toolbox, considering various PMU fault probabilities. The parameters are set as $h_i = 1$, $\Gamma_i = 0.12$, and $\Delta P_{L_i}(k) = 0.06e^{-0.05k}(\text{rand}(1) - 0.5)$.

Area 1	Area 2	Area 3	Area 4	Unit
$D_1 = 5$	$D_2 = 1$	$D_3 = 3$	$D_4 = 4$	pu/Hz
$2H_1 = 20$	$2H_2 = 14$	$2H_3 = 11$	$2H_4 = 9$	$pu \cdot s$
$T_{ch_1} = 1.2$	$T_{ch_2} = 1.0$	$T_{ch_3} = 0.7$	$T_{ch_4} = 0.5$	s
$T_{g_1} = 1.2$	$T_{g_2} = 0.6$	$T_{g_3} = 1.4$	$T_{g_4} = 0.8$	s
$R_1 = 0.016$	$R_2 = 0.03$	$R_3 = 0.05$	$R_4 = 0.08$	Hz/pu
$T_{12} = 0.1$	$T_{21} = 0.1$	$T_{31} = 0.1$	$T_{41} = 0.1$	pu/rad
$T_{13} = 0.1$	$T_{23} = 0.1$	$T_{32} = 0.1$	$T_{42} = 0.1$	pu/rad
$T_{14} = 0.1$	$T_{24} = 0.1$	$T_{34} = 0.1$	$T_{43} = 0.1$	pu/rad

Table 2.
Parameters of the four-area smart grid.

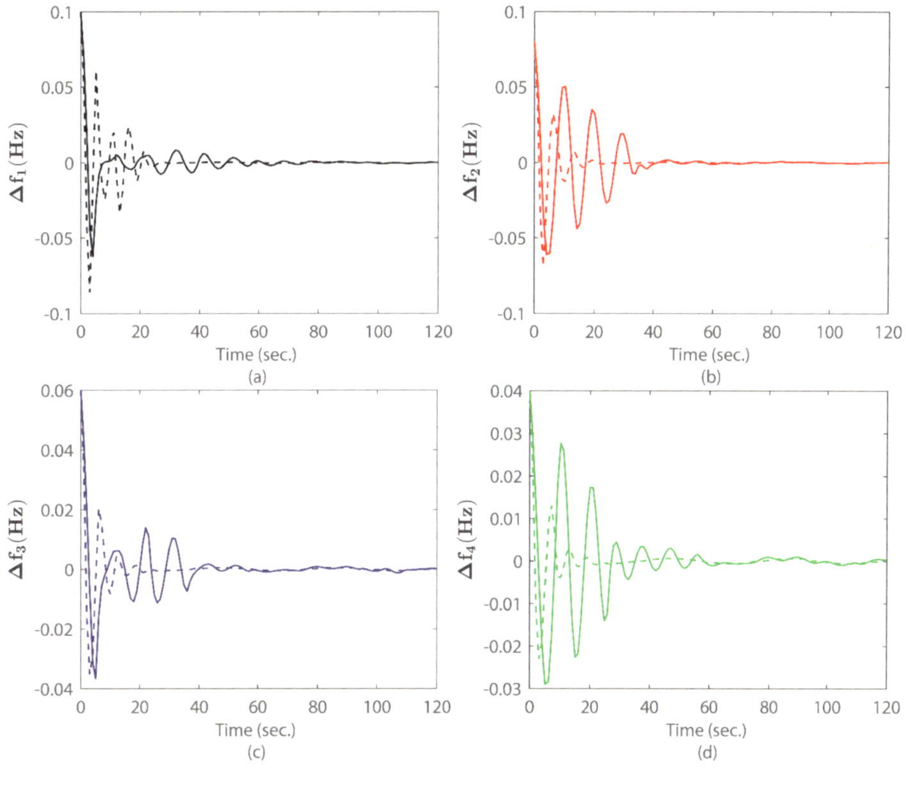

Figure 1.
Dynamics of Δf_i under traditional controller (solid lines) and under risk-mitigation controller (dotted lines) against PMU fault probability $1 - \overline{\theta}_i = 0.1$.

Figures 1 and **2** compare the dynamics of Δf_i between the traditional controller and the proposed risk-mitigation controller against PMU fault probabilities of $1 - \overline{\theta}_i = 0.1$ and 0.3. The results indicate that the proposed risk-mitigation controller consistently outperforms the traditional controller, although the extent of improvement varies across scenarios. The incorporation of the first risk-mitigation layer significantly reduces the settling time for each area. In summary, by considering different

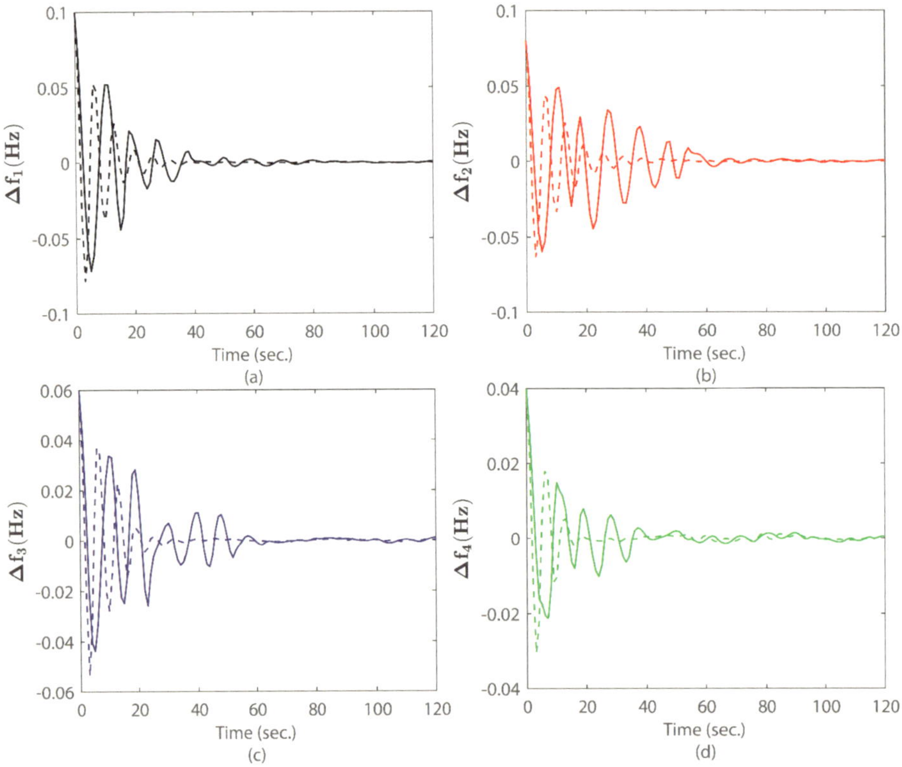

Figure 2.
Dynamics of Δf_i under traditional controller (solid lines) and under risk-mitigation controller (dotted lines) against PMU fault probability $1 - \overline{\theta}_i = 0.3$.

PMU fault probabilities during the offline control parameter configuration, the controller's resilience to PMU faults is enhanced. This validates the feasibility and effectiveness of the first risk-mitigation layer.

5.3 Second risk-mitigation layer validation

To validate the effectiveness of the second risk-mitigation layer, which focuses on online cyber attack detection within the communication network, the parameters for the decentralized model-based χ^2 detection mechanism is specified as follows: $\Gamma_j = 20$, $\Phi_j = \text{Diag}\{1, 1\}$, $G_j = \text{Diag}\{1, 0\}$, and $\delta_j = 10$. For demonstration purposes, we assume that the communication link from Area 3 to Area 2 is subjected to the FDI attacks characterized by $g_2(k) = [0.5 + 0.015k \quad 0]^T$ starting from $k = 50$.

Figure 3 compares the dynamics of Δf_i with and without the proposed intrusion detection unit. Without the online cyber attack detection unit, all four areas become unstable under FDI attacks, with Area 2 showing the most significant divergence due to cyber attacks on the communication link from Area 3 to Area 2. The other areas exhibit slower divergence influenced by the state updates from Area 2. With the deployment of the model-based χ^2 intrusion detection unit, the FDI attacks are promptly identified at $t = 57$s. Subsequently, implementing an attacked data compensation scheme based on the decentralized state estimation model (20), all four areas swiftly return to stable

DOI: http://dx.doi.org/10.5772/intechopen.1006719

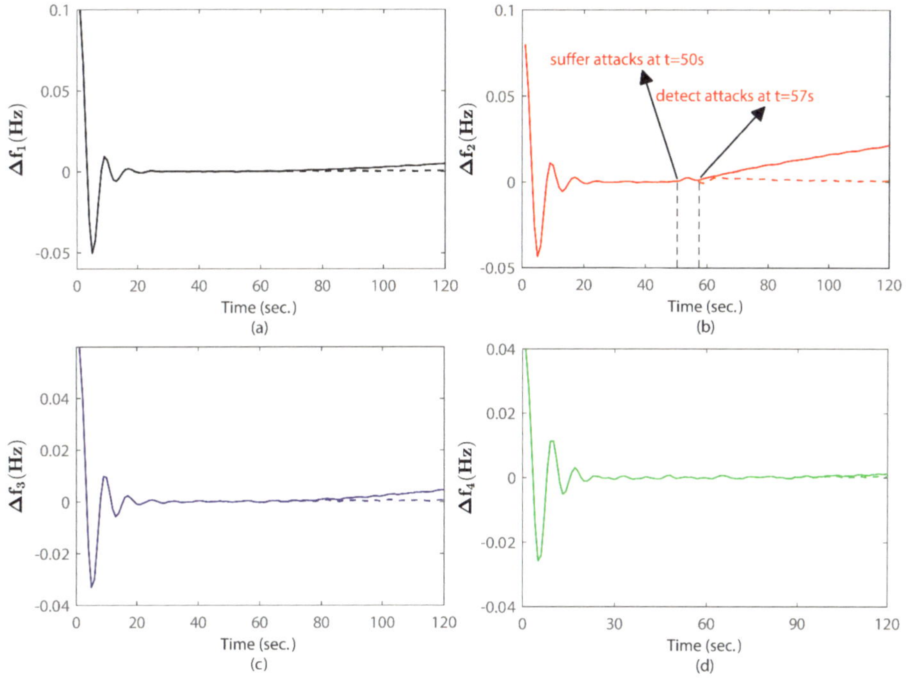

Figure 3.
Solid lines imply Δf_i without χ^2 detection unit while dotted lines imply Δf_i with χ^2 detection unit.

δ_2	FIR	FCR	ADT
90	0	0	88.60
75	0	0	69.11
60	0	0	48.86
30	0	0	28.24
15	0	0	8.15
10	0	0	5.54
6	2%	0	3.03
5	8%	0	2.79
3	14%	0	1.29
1	27%	0	1.00

Table 3.
KPIs under different δ_2.

states after a brief period of divergence. The extent of divergence and the detection time are closely related to the false alarm threshold δ_2. A larger δ_2 requires a longer detection time and results in greater divergence, and vice versa.

We also investigate the impacts of various δ_2 values (6, 15, 30, 45, 60) on Δf_2 under the given FDI attacks, and similar conclusions are drawn. We conduct 100 independent tests to obtain statistical results between a wider range of alarming thresholds δ_2 and the Key Performance Indicator (KPIs), as shown in **Table 3**.

Observant readers may note that the FCR remains zero even when δ_2 values as large as 90 are used. This occurs because the time-varying FDI attack, characterized by $g_2(k) = 0.5 + 0.015k$, continually increases in amplitude over time. Consequently, the proposed χ^2 detection mechanism can identify such FDI attacks. However, a significant drawback is the extended detection duration, resulting in a more pronounced divergence in frequency deviation dynamics. **Table 3** aims to serve as a guide for researchers and practitioners, providing references for balancing the FIR, FCR, and ADT.

6. Conclusions

This chapter proposes a dual-layer security framework addressing cyber-physical aspects within the context of IoT systems in smart grids. This framework enhances data utilization in smart grids under conditions of cyber-physical generalized uncertainties, such as sensor faults and cyber attacks. It introduces a novel approach to facilitate data collection and utilization under imperfect conditions and offers a valuable reference for researchers and practitioners in the fields of smart grids. Validation results confirm the feasibility and effectiveness of the proposed cyber-physical security framework for smart grids.

Acknowledgements

This work is supported in part by the A*STAR under its IAF-ICP Programme I2001E0067 and the Schaeffler Hub for Advanced Research at NTU, in part by National Research Foundation of Singapore under its Medium-Sized Center for Advanced Robotics Technology Innovation and by Naval Group Far East Pte Ltd via an RCA with NTU.

Author details

Zhijian Hu* and Rong Su*
Nanyang Technological University, Singapore

*Address all correspondence to: huzhijian1991@gmail.com; rsu@ntu.edu.sg

References

[1] Li J, Cheng Y. Deep meta-reinforcement learning-based data-driven active fault tolerance load frequency control for islanded microgrids considering internet of things. IEEE Internet of Things Journal. 2024;**11**(6):10295-10303

[2] Li Y, Zhang H, Liang X, Huang B. Event-triggered-based distributed cooperative energy management for multienergy systems. IEEE Transactions on Industrial Informatics. 2019;**15**(4): 2008-2022

[3] Zhang P, Zhang J, Yang J, Gao S. Resilient event-triggered adaptive cooperative fault-tolerant tracking control for multiagent systems under hybrid actuator faults and communication constraints. IEEE Transactions on Aerospace and Electronic Systems. 2023;**59**(3): 3021-3037

[4] Hu Z, Zhang K, Su R, Wang R. Robust cooperative load frequency control for enhancing wind energy integration in multi-area power systems. IEEE Transactions on Automation Science and Engineering. DOI: 10.1109/TASE.2024. 3367030

[5] Gao Z, Song Y, Wen C. Asymptotic tracking control with bounded performance index for MIMO systems: A neuroadaptive fault-tolerant proportional-integral solution. IEEE transactions on. Cybernetics. July 2024; **54**(7):4255-4266

[6] Ding K, Zhu Q, Huang T. Partial-information-based non-fragile intermittent estimator for microgrids with semi-aperiodic DoS attacks: Gain stochastic float. IEEE Transactions on Power Systems. 2024; **39**(1):2271-2283

[7] Hallaji E, Razavi-Far R, Wang M, Saif M, Fardanesh B. A stream learning approach for real-time identification of false data injection attacks in cyber-physical power systems. IEEE Transactions on Information Forensics and Security. 2022;**17**:3934-3945

[8] Roy DS, Murthy C, Mohanta DK. Reliability analysis of phasor measurement unit incorporating hardware and software interaction failures. IET Generation, Transmission & Distribution. 2015;**9**(2):164-171

[9] Zhang K, Zhijian H, Song F, Yang X, Liu Y. Consensus of input constrained multi-agent systems by dynamic time-varying event-triggered strategy with a designable minimal inter-event time. IEEE Transactions on Circuits and Systems II: Express Briefs. 2024;**71**(4): 2119-2123

[10] Duan T, Dinavahi V. Fast path recovery for single link failure in SDN-enabled wide area measurement system. IEEE Transactions on Smart Grid. 2022; **13**(2):1645-1653

[11] Zhijian H, Liu S, Luo W, Ligang W. Resilient distributed fuzzy load frequency regulation for power systems under cross-layer random denial-of-service attacks. IEEE Transactions on Cybernetics. 2022;**52**(4):2396-2406

[12] Xiao S, Dong J. Distributed fault-tolerant containment control for linear heterogeneous multiagent systems: A hierarchical design approach. IEEE Transactions on Cybernetics. 2022;**52**(2): 971-981

[13] Liu S, Zhijian H, Wang X, Ligang W. Stochastic stability analysis and control of secondary frequency regulation for islanded microgrids under random

denial of service attacks. IEEE Transactions on Industrial Informatics. 2019;**15**(7):4066-4075

[14] Zeyuan X, Wang D, Yi G, Zhijian H. Asynchronous tracking control of amplitude signals in vibratory gyroscopes with partially unknown mode information. IEEE Transactions on Industrial Electronics. 2023;**70**(7): 7478-7487

[15] Zhijian H, Rong S, Zhang K, Zeyuan X, Ma R. Resilient event-triggered model predictive control for adaptive cruise control under sensor attacks. IEEE/CAA Journal of Automatica Sinica. 2023;**10**(3):807-809

[16] Ma R, Zhijian H, Yang H, Jiang Y, Huo M, Luo H, et al. Adversarial FDI attack monitoring: Toward secure defense of industrial electronics. IEEE Industrial Electronics Magazine. June 2024;**18**(2):48-57

[17] Zhijian H, Liu S, Luo W, Ligang W. Intrusion-detector-dependent distributed economic model predictive control for load frequency regulation with pevs under cyber attacks. IEEE Transactions on Circuits and Systems I: Regular Papers. 2021;**68**(9):3857-3868

[18] Zhijian H, Rong S, Ling K-V, Guo Y, Ma R. Resilient event-triggered MPC for load frequency regulation with wind turbines under false data injection attacks. IEEE Transactions on Automation Science and Engineering. 2023. DOI: 10.1109/TASE.2023.3337006

[19] Zeng W, Chow M-Y. A reputation-based secure distributed control methodology in D-NCS. IEEE Transactions on Industrial Electronics. 2014;**61**(11):6294-6303

[20] Zhijian H, Liu S, Luo W, Ligang W. Credibility-based secure distributed load frequency control for power systems under false data injection attacks. IET Generation, Transmission & Distribution. 2020;**14**(17):3498-3507

[21] Yan J-J, Yang G-H, Wang Y. Dynamic reduced-order observer-based detection of false data injection attacks with application to smart grid systems. IEEE Transactions on Industrial Informatics. 2022;**18**(10):6712-6722

[22] Zhang K, Rong S, Zhang H, Tian Y. Adaptive resilient event-triggered control design of autonomous vehicles with an iterative single critic learning framework. IEEE Transactions on Neural Networks and Learning Systems. 2021; **32**(12):5502-5511

[23] Hu Z, Ma R, Wang B, Huang Y, Su R. A general resiliency enhancement framework for load frequency control of interconnected power systems considering internet of things faults. IEEE Transactions on Industrial Informatics. DOI: 10.1109/TII.2024. 3397400

[24] Zhijian H, Rong S, Wang R, Liu G, Zhang K, Xie X. Robust distributed load frequency control for multiarea wind energy-dominated microgrids considering phasor measurement unit failures. IEEE Internet of Things Journal. 2024;**11**(13):23475-23484